Successful
Sales
Management

The Institute of Management (IM) is at the forefront of management development and best management practice. The Institute embraces all levels of management from students to chief executives. It provides a unique portfolio of services for all managers, enabling them to develop skills and achieve management excellence.

If you would like to hear more about the benefits of membership, please write to Department P, Institute of Management, Cottingham Road, Corby NN17 1TT.

This series is commissioned by the Institute of Management Foundation.

SMARTER SOLUTIONS

The performance pack

Successful Sales Management

How to Make Your Team the Best

GRANT STEWART

London • New York • Toronto • Sydney • Tokyo • Singapore •
Madrid • Mexico City • Munich • Paris

PEARSON EDUCATION LIMITED

Head Office:
Edinburgh Gate
Harlow CM20 2JE
Tel: +44 (0)1279 623623
Fax: +44 (0)1279 431059

London Office:
128 Long Acre
London WC2E 9AN
Tel: +44 (0)207 447 2000
Fax: +44 (0)207 240 5771
www.business-minds.com

First published in Great Britain in 1996

© Pearson Education Limited 2000

The right of Grant Stewart to be identified as author of this work has been asserted by him in accordance with the Copyright, Designs, and Patents Act 1988.

ISBN 0 273 64488 2

British Library Cataloguing in Publication Data
A CIP catalogue record for this book can be obtained from the British Library.

10 9 8 7 6 5 4 3 2 1

Typeset by Northern Phototypesetting Co. Ltd, Bolton
Printed and bound in Great Britain by Biddles Ltd, Guildford and King's Lynn

The Publishers' policy is to use paper manufactured from sustainable forests.

Contents

Preface

Sales management is a particularly difficult job as it is one of the few relationships in business where the Manager rarely sees the staff. It is usually management at a distance. This often creates motivation and morale problems in the sales team.

At the same time competition is increasing in all markets as supply outpaces demand and products and services can be quickly copied. Supply is increasingly international so Sales Managers cannot just worry about domestic competition.

Many industries in all countries have been deregulated or privatised, and many government and charity bodies have been forced to become more sales-orientated. The demand for better and better customer service standards, promoted through growing consumer choice, has made even Governments promote 'Citizens' Charters' and customer service standards.

The sales force is vitally concerned with all these new developments. In some industries (eg financial services companies, notably banks and building societies), thousands of new Sales Managers have been appointed, often by converting existing staff into new job roles within a short time.

With such an important job to do, it is disappointing to see so many Sales Managers poorly recruited, trained and motivated to perform very complex job roles. The desire to write this book arose from two observations through consultancy and tailored training work with thousands of Sales Managers and hundreds of companies over many years.

1 A majority of Managers are not practising methods used by highly successful Sales Managers. Indeed, they often use methods which demotivate the team rather than motivate it to perform.

2 Books and publications on the subject sometimes fail to emphasise some very important processes and skills.

In particular this book aims to emphasise the importance in successful sales management of:

(a) Working with the team members to involve them in decision making and utilise their creative energies.

(b) Adapting the right management style consistent with the needs of the team and the Sales Manager's own personality.

(c) Trying to change Company culture and behaviour norms where they have become inappropriate to current and future needs.

(d) Judging all sales management actions by their ability to motivate desirable behaviour and attitudes in the sales team.

Purpose of the book

This book aims to provide very practical guidance to help Sales Managers adopt winning approaches to each of the key functions of the job. The content is based on best practice ideas and is consistent with research work in Excellence in company management.

It describes methods which work in *most* situations for *most* Managers and most teams. There are always exceptions, of course, but the reader is encouraged to try some new approaches, in the belief that failures can be reduced and successes increased.

The book encourages self-honesty, and open feedback from sales team members. The acid test for all Sales Managers is to ask team members how they feel the Manager is doing the job. Very few ever do this, but without honest feedback, progress is hard to achieve and old behaviours hard to change.

The book focuses on the 'people management' role of Sales Managers. It excludes most of the 'doing' role, which for some Sales Managers will include such jobs as sales administration, internal department liaison and promotional planning. It also excludes the sales processes which are functional skills of the sales team they are managing, eg selling steps and methods, key customer management and customer relationship management.

Who should read it

The book is designed for all who manage a sales team, either full time or as part of a broader job role. It is particularly aimed at first-line Sales Managers who may need to discard bad habits and discover new ones before it is too late.

Typical job titles with an interest in this book would be:

- Area/District/Regional Sales Managers.
- Field Sales Managers.
- National Sales Managers.
- Branch Managers (eg in banks, building societies, insurance companies).
- General Managers, with sales management as part of their role.
- Sales people who aspire to Sales Management.
- Marketing Managers, who need to liaise with the sales force.
- Sales Support Managers, who provide services to the sales force.
- Students of sales management, as part of a course or professional qualification.

Senior Sales Managers (eg Sales Directors, General Sales Managers, Sales and Marketing Directors) should also find the book of value, as their styles influence heavily the styles of their Managers. Little change is possible unless 'the Boss' supports and approves of the methods to be used, and 'the Boss' needs to coach the Sales Manager. Who coaches the coach?

The contents can be relevant to any country or culture, although some processes and behaviours will differ in certain countries. The skills of sales management, like those of selling, are universal and can be applied to any situation where products (industrial or consumer) or services are sold.

How to use the book

The book is structured against the main job roles of Sales Managers. It aims to provide challenge to existing practices for each task, and the reader is encouraged to compare current behaviour against practices suggested, and to try new approaches where appropriate. There are many creative ways to implement some of the broad ideas given, so experimentation is necessary. Try new ideas, review their effectiveness, try again. Keep being innovative.

Finally, any book can only hope to develop knowledge and help to change attitudes. It cannot develop skill; that only comes from doing, not reading. Constant practice has enormous benefits in improving sales management skills, through training, coaching and self-learning. Knowledge that is not used is useless. The more you practise, the luckier you get!

Acknowledgements

Many companies and Sales Managers have contributed to the contents of this book through our work in consultancy and tailored training over many years.

Particular thanks are due to Ashridge Management College, for whom I helped to develop and conduct a Field Sales Management Training Programme for nearly 10 years. We now conduct an open sales management programme previously licensed by Ashridge, and much gratitude is due to staff there for their support and use of research materials. Thanks are due to Peter Beddowes, Martyn Brown, Roger Pudney, Malcolm Schofield, Jorgen Petersen and Virginia Merritt of Ashridge for permission to reproduce materials developed for the Field Sales Management Programme. I would particularly like to thank Bob Ferdinand and Barry Paterson, with whom I have worked on the open programmes, for their contributions on the behavioural and management style aspects of sales management.

Thanks are also due to Steve Ingham of Michael Page Marketing for his help in the 'Recruitment' chapter, and to Mike Wilson, former Chairman of Marketing Improvements, for allowing extracts from his book *Managing a Sales Force* to appear in various chapters.

Finally, many thanks are due to my wife, Christine, who converted my spidery writing into the manuscript, and got it ready for the publishing deadline.

GRANT STEWART

Langham Management Consultants, 11 Curzon Avenue, Beaconsfield, Bucks HP9 2NN, Tel +44 (0) 1494 672001, Fax +44 (0) 1494 678037, email langham@clara.co.uk, website www.langham.clara.net

CHAPTER ONE

The sales management job

The aim of sales management is to achieve planned business development results by motivating the sales team members to perform to the best of their ability. Sales management, like selling, is a relentless and repetitive process.

This simple definition has a strong implication for the route to success in sales management - that the more time spent with the sales team, the better the results will be.

Many Sales Managers spend too little time with individual team members and with the team as a whole. Of the standard sales management tasks:

- Planning
- Organising
- Control
- Recruitment
- Training
- Motivation.

the ones with highest leverage on results are the 'people tasks' of training and motivation. They are particularly important because those managed are not seen daily (unlike most management jobs). Selling is lonely and poor people-management produces demotivation and poor performance.

The Problem

There are a number of reasons why many Sales Managers under-resource the people skills of the job.

1 **Personality**

Promoting the 'best Sales Person' to Sales Manager often courts disaster, as rarely do the qualities needed for good selling translate to those needed for good management.

Good sales representatives often have strong ego drive and a selfish desire to succeed. It is a lonely job, needing strong gifts of discipline and organisation.

Successful Sales Managers need to have a strong inclination to develop and support individuals and the sales team, often sublimating their own ego in the process. They should preferably like 'people' rather than 'things'.

The result of poor selection, rationalised as 'We had to promote our best sales person, otherwise how do we provide a promotion route?' can be disastrous - a Manager who does not feel comfortable in the job, and a team demotivated and neglected. A good sales person has been lost and a poor Manager recruited.

If possible, it is best to keep good sales personnel in selling (eg key accounts), while selecting competent sales representatives who show good 'people qualities' as Sales Managers. Managers must command respect, and thus must be competent at selling, but not necessarily the best. Many Sales Managers are just the wrong people for the job.

2 **Preferences**

People generally do what they like doing, which is not necessarily what needs to be done. If they prefer 'things' to 'people' they will spend most time doing those things, eg personal selling, administration, control. This means less time for people management, hence less motivation and morale building.

3 **Company tasks**

The Sales Manager is a bridge between the sales force and the rest of the Company. It is easy to be diverted into many tasks which are not directly relevant to the job of sales management, eg work on committees and working groups; internal meetings; Company politics; product development.

While these tasks are not unimportant, they are not as important as the motivation of the sales team.

4 **The Boss**

Many Sales Managers comment that they would love to spend more time with the sales team, but 'the Boss' does not see that as a priority against other, often internal, tasks.

Many senior Managers and Sales Directors have egos and personalities which are not very people-orientated. This is often a function of being brought up in a different management style and culture. It is often very hard for a Sales Manager to adopt a different approach to managing the team.

5 **Company culture**

A major influence on the Sales Manager and the adopted management style is the culture of the Company. Culture is the set of values describing the way the Company behaves, eg authoritarian/democratic; people/task orientated; warm/cold; conservative/experimental; caring/uncaring; trusting/suspicious; centralised/empowered.

These values usually spring from the Chief Executive and Board of Management, and often dictate the way new Managers carry out their job. It would be very difficult for a new Sales Manager to manage in a caring, empowered way if the Company culture was autocratic and valued people poorly.

Managing versus Doing

It is worthwhile for any Sales Manager to list tasks carried out in an average month, and to categorise each task by 'Managing' (M) or 'Doing' (D), as the following example shows:

D **(a)** Calling on an account with one of your sales team to show a customer that Company management is interested in the account.

M **(b)** Making a sales presentation to a prospective customer in order to show one of your sales team how to do it.

D **(c)** Making an independent call on an officer of a large account in order to cement customer relationships and promote business.

M **(d)** Explaining how to solve a work problem which one of your people has just brought to you.

D **(e)** Filling out a form to recommend a salary increase for a member of your department.

M **(f)** Explaining to one of your people a salary increase.

D **(g)** Interviewing a prospective salesperson referred to you by an employment agency.

M **(h)** Giving a telephone report of progress to your superior.

M **(i)** Asking one of your sales team what he or she thinks about a selling idea you have.

D **(j)** Planning and deciding on an objective by account.

M **(k)** Deciding what the cost budget request shall be for your sales office.

M **(l)** Reviewing monthly sales reports to determine progress toward specific sales objectives.

M **(m)** Deciding whether to meet a competitive price based on considerations beyond what the sales team member has access to.

M **(n)** Deciding whether to recommend adding a position.

D **(o)** Drafting an improved sales office layout.

M **(p)** Asking your sales team to establish tentative six-month objectives for the number of personal sales calls to be made on target accounts.

D **(q)** Giving a talk about your company's progress and plans to a local club or association.

M **(r)** Transferring an account from salesperson A to salesperson B because salesperson A did not devote the necessary effort to develop the account.

D **(s)** Phoning a plant manager to request help in solving a customer delivery problem for one of your sales team.

M **(t)** Planning the extent to which your sales team should use staff services during the next year to accomplish overall sales objectives.

The questions to ask are:

■ 'Are we paid to Manage or Do?'

■ 'How can we Manage more?'

Time Allocation

The next step is to carry out a Time Allocation, by trying to estimate time spent on activities grouped into main categories for an average month, as in this example:

	Activity	Sales Manager 1 Days per month (actual)	Sales Manager 2 Days per month (actual)	Days per month (desired)
1	Selling	5	–	
2	Internal meetings	2	1	
3	Sales team meetings	1	2	
4	Administration	2	1	
5	Committees	2	1	
6	Projects	2	2	
7	Coaching team	1	7	
8	Problem solving	2	1	
9	Planning	2	2	
10	Counselling	1	3	
		20	20	20

(please complete this column)

The activities vary from sales force to sales force, but in this example Sales Manager 1 is a typical 'Doer', spending only three days per month with the team (items 3,7,10) compared with 12 days on the same items for Sales Manager 2.

Of course, all Company circumstances are different, but the points made under 'The Problem' above have a major influence on time allocation.

As a rule of thumb, good Sales Managers spend up to **75 per cent** of their time with their team, either individually, or collectively. They plan to do this by the following rationale:

Activity	Rationale
1 COACHING	Improves knowledge, skills, and attitudes. Needs at least one day per person per month to be effective (more for new sales people); therefore **six to eight days per month** for average sales team.
2 SALES MEETINGS	Develops morale and team working, helps problem solving, and is an opportunity for group training. Needs at least **one full day per month, preferably two** to include training/problem solving.
3 COUNSELLING/ INDIVIDUAL MOTIVATION	A vital part of motivation. Needs regular attention to understand problems and help each member. Needs **two or three days per team per month**.
4 COMMUNICATION	Important for team building and recognition, verbal and written. Needs creativity, and should absorb **two days per team per month**.
5 APPRAISAL/CAREER DEVELOPMENT	Should be much more than annual, as regular as quarterly, ie up to **one day per month per team**.
6 SALES PLANNING/ ANALYSIS	Needs to be participative for greatest motivation. Should be about **one day per month per team**, concerned with goal setting and action plans.

All these activities require about 75 per cent of a Sales Manager's available time, or **15 days per month**. Managing the sales force in this people-orientated way increases leverage on performance significantly, which more than justifies the time spent.

Time Productivity

The only way more time with the team can be found is to lose time elsewhere. This is an eternal time-management problem, and Sales Managers must make a savage attack on all their unproductive and low-leverage uses of time.

The way to achieve this is to classify all activities as follows:

'A' – *Essential activities*, particularly those concerned with motivating the sales team and sales performance.

'B' – *Desirable activities*, lower impact on team and sales performance.

'C' – *Non-desirable activity*, minor impact on job performance.

If time productivity is to be improved, the Sales Manager should operate the '3Ds' approach:

Do 'B' and 'C' category activities fast, spending little time on each one. Budget the time, and stick to it.

Delegate 'B' and 'C' category activities to other team members, administrative staff or others in the Company. Delegation increases responsibility and motivates staff, and can release significant time for the Sales Manager. Good managers are good delegators, poor ones take on too many 'monkeys'.

Dump some 'C' category activities altogether, or just do them less frequently. The question to ask is: If this activity was not done at all, would it affect the business adversely? As an example, a Senior Manager in a large company forgot to send in a monthly return one month. He found nobody asked him for it, so his policy became to send in the return only every other month - nobody ever noticed, and he has done this for many years! Be a renegade not a slave to procedures which may have outlived their usefulness.

Also, make more use of the waste paper basket!

Do you manage your time, or does time manage you? Spend more time with the sales team, and it will be well rewarded.

CHECKPOINTS

- How close are you to 75% of your time with the people?
- How can you create more time for people management?
- By what criteria do you select Sales Managers in your Company?

CHAPTER TWO

Motivation

What is motivation?

Motivation is what makes a person do something, and what makes him/her put real effort and energy into what he/she does. It varies in nature and intensity from individual to individual, depending on the particular mixture of influences at any given moment.

SIMPLE DEFINITION:
Getting people to do willingly and well those things which have to be done

It has been stated that:

■ Positive motivation occurs when people 'give' to a request.

■ Motivation ceases when people are 'compelled' to surrender to a demand. Try to obtain commitment by involvement, not by fear or by your own status alone.

The importance of motivation

Motivation is vital for an individual to give of his/her best. Assuming that employees are given opportunity for good performance and have the necessary skills, then effectiveness depends on their motivation.

Research evidence through sales staff feedback methods (see Chapter 10) shows that motivation is consistently the most important requirement by the sales force of their Sales Manager. Success in this area of skill will give the Sales Manager a clear route to effectiveness.

Signs of motivation

The attitudes and behaviour of the sales force often reflect motivation or the lack of it. Examples of the signs of motivation are:

- High performance and results being consistently achieved.
- The energy, enthusiasm and determination to succeed.
- Unstinting co-operation in overcoming problems.
- The willingness of individuals to accept responsibility.
- Willingness to accommodate necessary change.

Lack of motivation

Conversely, employees who are demotivated or who lack motivation often display:

- Apathy and indifference to the job.
- A poor record of time-keeping and high absenteeism.
- An exaggeration of the effects/difficulties encountered in problems, disputes and grievances.
- A lack of co-operation in dealing with problems or difficulties.
- Unjustified resistance to change.

Sales Managers generally deplore lack of motivation and interest in the Company and in work. Many men and women turn their excess energies and talents to hobbies and merely tolerate their jobs as a way of earning their living so they can afford to meet the challenge of life in leisure-time activities. It is not leisure as a pursuit, but work as a drudgery, that is to be condemned.

Repetitive, monotonous and uninteresting selling jobs can be made more palatable if Managers recognise the rights of individuals. Countless others have the elements of challenge and interest in them destroyed by Managers' failure to recognise human needs and motivations.

Understanding motivation

Sales Managers should carry out the following exercise at regular intervals:

For each member of the sales team, write down the three main **motivators** in priority order, and the three main **demotivators**. Then ask each sales team member to do the same.

If there is a significant difference between your judgement and the self-assessment of the team members, you are probably not close enough to individuals or the team as a whole. Close understanding of what motivates or demotivates individuals is the key to effectiveness as a motivator.

Do not be afraid to *ask* about motivation regularly, eg at every coaching visit or sales meeting. Try to be open about motivation, and do not be afraid to address any factor which affects motivation, including personal problems, relationships within the team, or your own management style. Frankness and closeness breed respect and understanding.

Also, when was the last time your boss talked to you about *your* motivation?

The research on motivation

Over the years, a growing number of behavioural scientists have carried out their own investigations into what makes people 'tick'. It would be wrong to ignore this accumulated knowledge, but equally wrong to pretend that each viewpoint in itself holds the key to solving our problems of motivating people. The results and findings of some, however, do give an insight of practical significance which can be helpful to the understanding of the line manager.

Douglas McGregor (quoting A. H. Maslow) suggests that people's needs can be depicted in a kind of hierarchy (Fig. 2.1). At the bottom of the triangle are the needs of our animal nature for self-preservation – for sleep, food and water, for shelter and warmth. These needs are basic; as someone aptly said, 'Man does not live by bread alone, except when there is no bread.' Once satisfied, they cease to be strong motivators to action.

Thus as Western man begins to feel more materially secure, his higher needs for self-expression (including the drive for achievement), for an objective, for self-fulfilment, clamour for satisfaction. It follows, therefore, that in suitable circumstances and with proper management, the majority of people can be self-directed if they become

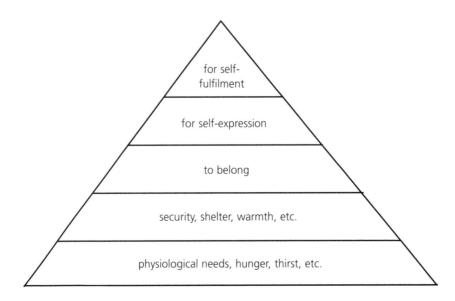

Figure 2.1

Source: 'Hierarchy of Needs', from *Motivation and Personality*, by Abraham H. Maslow. Copyright 1954 by Harper and Row, Publishers, Inc. Copyright 1970 by Abraham H. Maslow. Reprinted by permission of Harper Collins Publishers.

committed to an objective they value. They will not only accept responsibility, but often will seek it. Furthermore, to work is as natural as to eat or to sleep. Creativity is widely, not narrowly, scattered among the population. (This is McGregor's 'Theory Y'.)

In short, people can be self-motivated. The task of the manager is to create conditions of work in which, and through which, self-motivation can find its release. In situations where this is difficult to achieve – as in dull, repetitive work – higher pay remains of paramount importance, since workers are forced to find satisfaction outside the work situation. Managers can make assumptions about people at work. Extremes can be described as X and Y – see the X-Y theory illustrated in Table 2.1

If X is to be our assumption and we treat people accordingly, we find out nothing about them and our beliefs will become a self-fulfilling prophecy, ie people will need close supervision, firm discipline, incentive schemes, etc.

If, however, we believe that Y is correct and treat people accordingly, we shall find out what they are really like. The answer will be that they are all different and we can then manage them according to their strengths and weaknesses.

Table 2.1 The X-Y theory

Theory X	Theory Y
1 Man dislikes work and will avoid it if he can	1 Work is necessary to man's psychological growth
2 Man must be forced or bribed to put out the right effort	2 Man wants to be interested in his work and, under the right conditions, he can enjoy it
3 Man would rather be directed than accept responsibility, which he avoids	3 Man will direct himself towards an accepted target
	4 Man will seek, and accept, responsibility under the right conditions
	5 The discipline a man imposes on himself is more effective, and can be more severe, than any imposed on him
4 Man is motivated mainly by money	6 Under the right conditions man is motivated by the desire to realise his own potential
5 Man is motivated by anxiety about his security	
6 Most men have little creativity – except when getting round management rules	7 Creativity and ingenuity are widely except distributed and widely under-used

Source: McGregor's Theory X and Y, '*The Human Side of Enterprise*', McGraw Hill, 1960.

The key is in not making assumptions, but in giving opportunity for achievement, responsibility, creativity and using talent, abilities, interests, etc., in so far as the task allows.

Frederick Herzberg asked many people in different jobs at different levels to consider two things:

> 'Describe a time when you felt very good about your job'
> 'Describe a time when you felt very bad about your job'

After content analysis of these initial events by independent coders, two different sets of factors emerged. Fig. 2.2 summarises the order and frequency with which the factors appeared in the first 12 studies.

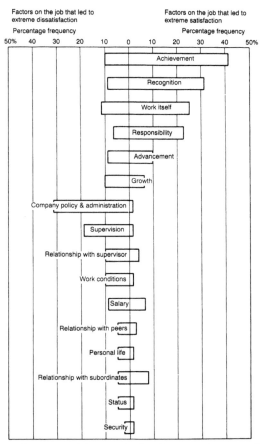

Figure 2.2   Percentage frequency of factors which affect attitudes to work

Source: Frederick Herzberg, 'One More Time: How Do You Motivate Employees?', *Harvard Business Review*, 1968.

1. Dissatisfaction

Factors on the left of the chart show a greater potential for dissatisfaction than satisfaction. Improving them or giving people more of them or better:

(a)   does not create a motivational atmosphere

(b)   creates only short-lived satisfaction, because they become accepted as the norm, eg a salary increase or new car might motivate for one month, but no more.

In Herzberg's words, 'You just remove unhappiness, you don't make people happy'.

These factors are connected with the job context. Herzberg called them the 'hygiene factors'.

2. Satisfaction

Factors on the right of the chart have little to do with money and status; much to do with achievement and responsibility. They are connected with the job content. Herzberg called them the 'motivators'.

Practical motivation

From this understanding of what motivates and demotivates the sales team members, Sales Managers need to adopt an *active* approach to motivation. When Sales Managers are asked how they allocate their time, as in Chapter 1, almost never does any time get allocated to motivation.

Yet to be a successful Sales Manager motivation must be active, not passive. It helps to like people and to be liked yourself, and it certainly helps to be charismatic, but if such qualities are lacking, the effort put in to practical motivation will be essential. Do not be lazy as a motivator. Work hard at it, and learn what works and does not work for individuals and the team.

An excellent way to produce active motivation is to write down *every day* answers to the following question: 'What have I done today to motivate or demotivate the sales team?' If you can write down nothing positive on balance, then you are not doing enough active motivation.

Ideas checklists

It is worthwhile to draw up a list of actions you can take to produce increased motivation, based on your assessment of what motivates individual team members and the team as a whole. First, try to remove as many demotivators as you can (consistent with Company policy), remembering that positive motivation follows satisfaction with the 'hygiene factors'. Sometimes you may need to take a risk and bend the rules to remove an obstacle to motivation.

If you follow the Herzberg motivational categories, you can quickly produce *40 or 50 ideas* (with some overlap between the categories) for practical motivation, all with endless creative variations.

Examples would be:

1 ACHIEVEMENT

- various sales targets (not just sales volume)
- performance standards (see Chapter 4)
- projects and exercises
- qualifications
- qualitative goals
- self-set targets/plans
- goal achievement reports/discussions

2 RECOGNITION

- more praise (regularly, by telephone, by letter, at meetings)
- less criticism
- token recognition (eg dinners, small gifts)
- incentives/rewards/prizes
- job titles/status (eg Senior Salesperson, Salesperson of the Month)
- graphs/league tables
- newsletters
- giving your time/availability
- salary increase/bonus
- regular communications/feedback

3 WORK ITSELF

- job clarity/description
- standards of performance, (published)
- variety (eg change accounts, even territories, occasionally)
- freedom to work their own way
- less boredom/routine
- pride/enthusiasm
- team spirit
- support for the job
- collective decisions

4 RESPONSIBILITY

- more job responsibility (eg to negotiate prices)
- more information (eg product profitability)
- market or customer development roles
- presentations at meetings
- training session at meetings
- organising trade event
- involvement in planning/own plan
- producing Sales Manual
- less supervision
- encouraging new ideas
- specialism

5 ADVANCEMENT/PERSONAL GROWTH

- career plan (eg 'fast-track' personnel)
- promotion
- status of job
- pay increase
- counselling (regularly)

- job/career objectives/plans
- training/self-improvement
- temporary team-leadership (eg holidays, meetings)
- meet personal needs (eg help in job skills or qualifications)
- job-transfer/experience/secondment
- training role for new sales people

The list can be modified and supplemented through experience, and should act as a constant catalyst to the Sales Manager to treat motivation as active, not passive.

The Herzberg checklist can be used to create motivational profiles for the sales force. This is done by selecting, in consultation with each sales person, factors which they feel affect their motivation. This can be done without prompting, or by using the Herzberg checklist, as given.

Each sales person can then be asked to score each factor (eg out of a 5 or 10 point scale) in terms of how each rates the importance to them of that factor and how it motivates them at present. The priorities given can then form the basis of the Sales Manager's active plan to deliver motivationally what each person requires, with feedback on motivational satisfaction on a regular basis.

1. Achievement (others can be done for the other Motivators)	Importance in Motivating You (1–5)	How Factor Motivates You at Present (1–5)
Sales targets		
performance standards		
projects and exercises		
qualifications		
qualitative goals		
self set targets/plans		
goal achievement reports/discussion		

Figure 2.3 Example of Motivational Profile Motivating Factor (from Herzberg list)

Motivating change

Change is normal. Change is an inherent part of life. Why then do all people constantly resist it?

Sir Barnes Wallis was once quoted as saying, 'We are all suspicious of other people's ideas'.

Can resistance to change be regarded as abnormal or pathological? One point of view holds that it is more a 'symptom' than a disease.

When resistance does appear it should not be thought of as something to be overcome. Instead it can best be thought of as a useful red flag – a signal that something is wrong.

Undoubtedly, one of the most challenging roles which a Sales Manager plays is that of motivating change in the sales team.

Implementing change is about starting, changing gear, stopping, accelerating, slowing down and arriving. The theme throughout is about involving others to be co-operative, willing and flexible. While you may not waver from your final objective, your activities and circumstances may change in the process of reaching that goal.

Symbolically we intend to make a triangle – circumstances demand a circle. Only with flexibility can we effect change.

Motivating and managing change requires:

- The full co-operation of all concerned in the business.
- An effective method of communication which is two-way at all stages and levels.
- Effective feedback to the decision-making centre of progress and obstacles.

Change has very often to be effected while maintaining present procedures and if this is to be achieved, it requires the full co-operation of the participants.

Gaining the willing consent throughout the course of effecting change is positive motivation.

Introducing change

Examples of change:

Major changes

- altering pay or bonus systems;
- introducing new organisations;
- making a major change in procedure.

Minor changes

- a new administration procedure;
- making a small alteration in working methods;
- modifying working practices.

Change is inevitable and is a continuing process. Even minor changes may have major repercussions; for what appears to be a minor change to the managers may seem a major one to the employees affected.

Why do people resist change?

They resist not because of the change itself, but because it means adjusting themselves to a changed situation, and because of fears such as:

- loss of job;
- loss of skills;
- inability to cope with change;
- loss of earnings;
- loss of status;
- loss of companions (owing to work reorganisation);
- loss of familiar surroundings.

How then should managers introduce change?

Communications and consultation are particularly important in times of change. The achievement of change is a joint concern of management and employees and should be carried out in a way which pays regard both to the efficiency of the undertaking and to the interests of employees. Major changes in working agreements should not be made by Management without prior discussion with employees or their representatives.

(a) Plan: taking into account who it will affect and how it will affect them.

(b) Explain: the need for change – by managers briefing down the line to all those affected.

(c) Consult those affected or their representatives:
- it tells them that their views are being considered, resulting in increased willingness to co-operate;
- it tells you of their specific anxieties, allowing you to take these problems into account;
- consultation may bring out important factors previously overlooked.

(d) Analyse ie consider and act on the results of consultations. In particular:
- reconsider your original plan;
- give reassurance of no redundancy or loss of earnings (when possible);
- take steps to provide training.

(e) Communicate the change, the reasons for it and its impact on those affected, by managers briefing down the line to all employees concerned, supporting this with adequate written information and/or instructions.

(f) Implement the change.

(g) Follow up to see that the change has proceeded as planned, and the objective achieved. Further consultation, readjustment and communication may be necessary.

Motivating through remuneration

Although many factors affect motivation, it is true to say that the Pay and Reward System drives behaviour because it shows how the Company rewards sales activity. Although Sales Managers rarely decide payment systems (often a Board decision), they can recommend a review of the current system.

The key factor is the *nature of the selling job*. If the selling job has:

- a high service element, not just order taking
- a long time to produce orders
- team effort in selling
- repeat order cycles

then salary should be a high proportion of total remuneration. If the opposite applies, then commission (either in money or in kind) will form a high proportion of total pay.

These differences are often described as 'soft sell' versus 'hard sell'. The problem arises where the Company wishes to promote service selling, but has a payment system encouraging 'hard' selling; or the reverse – where incentives are not high enough to encourage sales results.

Sometimes the imbalance is caused by a historical payment system not reflecting new market requirements. In one example, a major equipment company paid a high proportion of total pay in commission (averaging 40 per cent), while seeking to be a high quality of service supplier. The sales force had no encouragement to carry out repeat service calls (not rewarded), so customers became unhappy and complaints arose.

The sales force were asked if they would accept a higher basic salary, but a likely total remuneration reduction (less commission). Over 90 per cent said they would, provided their job titles were changed to increase their status with customers – a reflection on motivation values, as well as re-balancing the pay system.

Some problems

Many compensation schemes for sales staff are designed with the aim of encouraging improved performance through financial incentives. Whilst these can prove to be very effective some are of doubtful value for a variety of reasons:

- Perceived as being inequitable when comparing one salesperson's benefits with another's for similar work or sales results.

- The additional financial reward for increased effort is too low to provide any real motivation, or too high for the sales effort expended.

- It is difficult to directly relate increased effort to increased sales or profits.

- Commission scheme controls the operation of the sales force. Unwilling to change territories because of interfering with earnings potential.

- The commission is paid well after the increased effort has been made (eg annual bonuses) and is not seen as being directly related to it.

- Complexity of the mechanism for working out the commission payment.

- Basing the scheme simply on volume of business generated with no account of profitability.

- Rewarding the luck element too highly, eg a customer moves offices and places a large order in a new sales territory.

Criteria for commission payments

Where the marketing situation is conducive to paying sale staff in part by commission the following guidelines should be kept to if increased motivation is hoped for.

1 As far as possible the additional financial reward must be directly related to the skill and effort of each salesperson and not be greatly affected by conditions outside their control.

2 A reasonable proportion of the salesperson's total remuneration should be in the form of fixed salary. This amount should be enough to provide financial security.

3 The commission feedback period should be as short as practically possible.

4 The method of calculating payments should be understood by the sales force.

5 The commission rates payable must be high enough to act as a motivator without being uneconomic to the company.

6 The commission scheme should be designed so as to provide continuing incentives to both new and experienced salespeople.

Please score the following factors within your company Pay/Incentive system

	Factor	Score 1–10
1	Drives right sales behaviours	
2	Easy to understand	
3	Rewards success	
4	Salary level as proportion of pay	
5	Incentive level as proportion of pay	
6	Competitive within our industry	
7	Speed of incentive payment	
8	Fairness	
9	Rewards skill and effort	
10	Rewards profit, not just sales volume	

Figure 2.4 10 Factors for Scoring the Motivational Success of a Pay/Incentive System

Motivation exercises

1 Describe yourself through the eyes of each of your sales team members.
Would he/she be irritated or frustrated by any of your traits or actions?
What would be seen as your strong points?

2 Describe yourself through the eyes of your boss.
How could you appear to better advantage or be more fully understood?

3 List your sales team members and against them list their main dislikes or demotivating influences, and their main motivators.
Do you know them well enough to be reasonably sure you are right?

4 List six main causes of frustration in your operation and six causes of job satisfaction.

5 Apply the six rules to the work of your sales team and decide on at least three ways to improve motivation for each team member.

One final point. Motivating a sales team is very dependent on creating *enthusiasm*. If all the Sales Manager's actions are done with enthusiasm and fun, that will be infectious, and the reverse will be the case. Enthusiasm and motivation go hand in hand.

MOTIVATION CHECKLIST

1 **Ask** what motivates/demotivates (regularly)

2 Ask **how** you motivate/demotivate (staff questionnaire)

3 **Open** style – flat; honest; part of team; empathetic

4 **Involvement**/Empowerment/Communications

5 **Assertive/warm** style – fair

6 **Not fear**– create confidence
         – 'Feel-good' factor

7 **Friendly**, challenging culture

8 **Active** motivation (Herzberg checklist)

9 Strong **vision/core values**

10 **Coach**/helper

11 **Visible** – with the people

12 Always **enthusiastic**

CHECKPOINTS

- What motivates and demotivates each of your sales team?
- How can you improve actively the motivation of your sales force?
- How can you improve your personal motivational style of management?

Managem
style/cultu

Chapter 1 referred to potential barriers to succesful sales management, two of which were

- personality/management style
- company culture.

The style of management will often be influenced very strongly by Company culture, which in turn is usually influenced most strongly by the Chief Executive/Board.

Winning sales management cultures

Enlightened companies strive to be as salesperson orientated as possible. Companies who sincerely care about their people, train them properly, involve them in decision making, and support them with the best products, delivery and personal rewards and recognition, see sales go up and management skills improve.

Many of these approaches are similar to successful Japanese management practices. Although the Japanese are better known for their management and production practices, much of the world-wide Japanese success can be attributed to their marketing and sales management practices. Successful sales organisations are many, but the better-known companies follow practices similar to the Japanese. Successful firms emphasise customer service, rather than profits, in the short run. They take an overview that better quality products and service will generate profits in the long run.

seven S's of sales management

ractices of companies that are similar to the much talked about Japanese
ent practices are called 'the Seven S's.[1] The Seven S's can be broken down into
ategories: the three hard S's and the four soft S's. The three hard S's are **strategy**,
ructure and **systems**.

- **Strategy** places emphasis upon a salesperson's and Sales Manager's need for charted course of action, the practice of good time-management, and the allocation of their scarce resources over time, to best meet the identified goals and objectives of the sales organisation. The assignment of legitimate sales territories, the establishment of attainable sales quotas, proper training in sales practices, correct sales presentations, and the proper way to establish sales trip itineraries, all illustrate sales strategies.

- **Structure** refers to the way a firm is organised – whether it is centralised or decentralised, or whether it emphasises line or staff. The hierarchy of the line sales organisation and its relationship with staff or support areas, or how the organisation-boxes are arranged, represents the sales structure.

- **Systems** are represented by proceduralised reports, routine processes, meetings, policies, complaints, or reward systems. Examples of sales systems would be: returned goods policies; products storage and shipment; sales meetings at all levels; handling of sales orders; sales compensation; customer complaints; and sales recognition reward systems. So far, most firms are equal to, or surpass their Japanese counterparts in the three hard S's. It is within the four soft S's that a difference begins to appear, and where Japanese management practices may offer the most significant contribution to sales management.

The difficult soft S's are the areas that successful sales organisations should emphasise the most. These represent the personal concern, the caring for one another, and the emphasis placed on the human investment an organisation is willing to make. The soft S's are **staff, style, skills**, and **superordinate** goals.

---

[1] Waterman, Jr., Peters and Phillips, 'Structure is Not Organisation,' pp. 14-26. Reprinted from *Business Horizons*, 14-26 June 1980. Copyright 1980 by the Foundation for the School of Business at Indiana University. Used with permission.

- **Staff** is the demographic description of important personnel categories within the sales organisation, such as sales representative or territory manager, zone Sales Manager, branch manager and so on. Although these positions appear to be perfunctory, the successful firms, in line with the Japanese, treat these positions with honour, trust and respect.

- **Style** is the characterisation of how key managers behave in achieving the organisation's goals within the cultural context of the firm. A strong employee-orientated organisation would exhibit a caring attitude and build trust and respect among its people and managers. It would believe in the importance of each human being within the sales organisation, and in the potential contribution of each to that organisation. Management would encourage support, listening, employee involvement, and participative management.

- **Skills** represent the Company's willingness to spend money to adequately train each employee for the next assignment. Frequently, sales organisations spend much time training field sales representatives, but they spend only a day or two training a new or prospective Sales Manager in the art of managing people. Inadequate management training can encourage poor sales supervision, or worse yet, precipitate high salesperson turnover. The large investment in a 'newly quit' salesperson's training is lost, since it only benefits a competitive company or the person going into business for him or herself. Skill, at all levels, must be as effective and as efficient as possible. The luxury of assuming that a good salesperson will make a good manager without proper training has been refuted many times. Frequently, a good salesperson, without adequate management training, can make one of the worst Sales Managers.

- **Superordinate** goals have a significant meaning, since these are the guiding concepts with which a sales organisation imbues its members. At first glance, a hard-nosed salesperson may scoff at spiritual or inspirational overtones or with sharing values of other people within the organisation. Yet superordinate goals are one of the most important S's in successful sales organisations. These are not the important values of ROI, cost incurred, expected sales, or the market share goal, but are values that 'move hearts', and genuinely unite and bind together the individual and the organisation's purposes.

A computer salesperson realises the importance of making the sale, since a higher order of service to society is provided in making the sale. The computer buyer's cost of doing business can be decreased, and the efficiency can be increased to provide better products at lower prices to customers and society at large. Japanese cultural values dictate that business firms must demonstrate their products serve societal needs before society accepts them. This concept is strongly related to the marketing concept which focuses upon a strong consumer satisfaction orientation for all the firm's concerns.

Combining hard and soft S's

Some Sales Managers tend to focus on the three hard S's to achieve sales goals. Strategies, structure and systems can be quantified, analysed with cold logic, and be thought about conceptually. Examples of the emphasis on hard S's are: sales data print-outs; number of calls made; number of demonstrations; number of qualified leads; and hard-nosed no-nonsense questions, such as when the Sales Manager asks the Territory Manager at the close of a hard day, 'Well, what did you sell today?' These necessary S's by themselves, can be interpreted by salespeople as the uncaring attitudes of sales management. 'Sales Managers are only interested in the Company and their own advancement within the firm.'

The four soft S's, on the other hand, can be interpreted by salespeople as a concerned, caring, respectful attitude and as the Company's willingness to train and support the salesperson and the Sales Manager. The seventh and last S is exemplified by the Sales Manager who believes that each person in the organisation can and should believe that he or she is giving a valuable service to society, rather than just making a sale to enhance profits or present position. Making a sale creates one of the most exhilarating feelings a salesperson can experience, but this feeling is more motivational and lasting when the salesperson can appreciate the magnitude of service he or she has created in making the sale. For every sale made, not only is the product's service rendered to the outside society, but also gainful employment can be increased within the selling organisation.

Successful Sales Managers feel for and with their people, consult with them, care about them as human beings, and genuinely lead them by supporting them, assisting them, and informing them. A successful salesperson's relationship with a customer is to inform, to educate, and to enlighten in order to make a sale.

Why should it be any different for the Sales Manager when dealing with his or her own people to become a better supervisor and manager? Instead of a Sales Manager saying, 'What did you sell today?', how much better to say, 'How can I help you to be more productive?' This small change in attitude is a significant step toward more productive sales management, which can lead to more productive salespeople, and the generation of greater profits in the long run.

Salespeople and Sales Managers are no better than how they feel about their position, their products, their company, their societal worth, and their customers. A greater sense of need, trust, and respect among salespeople and Sales Managers frequently can override any pitfalls in a sales organisation's inadequate strategy, structure, or systems. The major strength of a sales organisation lies, not in its perfect strategies, but in its well-trained and motivated people.

Winning sales management styles

The model developed by Buzzotta, Lefton and Sherberg is an excellent way to analyse your own style, and consider the ways in which you might change your behaviour. Situations faced, company culture, and your own and team personalities, also influence the style to be adopted, but in general the style most likely to win in most situations through positive (not fear) motivation is: DOMINANT/WARM (QUADRANT 4)

DOMINANCE

Quadrant 1	**Quadrant 4**
Planning: Rarely involves salespeople ('Why should I? Planning is my prerogative. I make the plans, they carry them out. That's as it should be.')	*Planning*: Consults salespeople whenever their thinking might help ('I want the best plans possible. That frequently requires ideas from others. I don't have all the answers.')
Organising: Tight organisation. Patterns of relationship emphasise one-to-one interaction ('I make sure everyone knows what to do and how to do it. I call the shots.')	*Organising*: Patterns of relationship designed to stimulate collaboration and interdependence ('I try to get synergy through pooling of resources.')
Controlling: Very close supervision ('Any Sales Manager who isn't vigilant is asking for trouble. Salespeople must know they're closely scrutinised.')	*Controlling*: Tries to develop salespeople who control themselves. ('Get people committed to their goals and they'll supervise their own efforts.') Provides more structure for those who can't.
Leading: Pushes, demands, drives ('Most people want a strong leader to tell them what to do. My people know who's boss.')	*Leading*: Tries to make salespeople aware of their potential ('Leadership is helping people do what they have it in them to do. A leader develops people.')

HOSTILITY ——————————————————————— **WARMTH**

Quadrant 2	**Quadrant 3**
Planning: Relies heavily on own Manager ('I prefer to pass plans along. That way, my people know they'd better follow through') or leans heavily on tradition ('It's worked before, it should work again.')	*Planning*: More concerned with generalities than details ('If you fence people in with too much planning you'll demoralise them. I'm flexible. I give my people plenty of leeway'.)
Organising: Patterns of relationship vague, indefinite. Doesn't encourage interaction ('Just do your own job, and stay out of trouble.')	*Organising*: Patterns of relationship emphasise loosely structured sociability. ('If people feel good about their jobs, they'll do their best without lots of regulation. My job is to make sure they feel good.')
Controlling: Sees self mainly as a caretaker ('I'm paid to keep things stable. I exert enough control to make sure nobody disrupts routines. There's no point in doing more.')	*Controlling*: Relies on high morale to produce hard work. ('Control is secondary. What salespeople need most is a good feeling about their jobs.')
Leading: Passive, indifferent. Downplays own influence ('Don't kid yourself. No matter how hard you try to lead people, they'll end up doing pretty much as they please.')	*Leading*: Believes optimism and encouragement get results ('Being a Sales Manager is like being a cheerleader. You can't let your people get discouraged.')

SUBMISSION

Figure 3.1   Sales management styles

Source: V. R. Buzzotta, R. E. Lefton, Manuel Sherberg, from copyrighted publication of Psychological Associates Inc., St. Louis, Mo., which may not be reproduced without express permission of their UK representatives P.S.I. International, Arundel, West Sussex, England.

Management function	Quadrant 1	Quadrant 2	Quadrant 3	Quadrant 4
Basic attitude	Salespeople must be pushed	Salespeople are what they are	Salespeople produce when happy	Salespeople produce when involved and committed
Planning	Does it on own	Transmits from above	Makes popular plans	Strategically involves salespeople
Organising	Tightly controls operation	Goes by the book; interaction vague, minimal	Permissive, relatively unstructured	Optimal participation, autonomy, and responsibility for everyone
Controlling	Relies on fear and coercion	Leans on routines	Relies on permissive human relations	Fosters self-control through understanding
Leading	Drives and threatens	Indifferent, distant, unresponsive	Eager to please, appeases, smoothes over	Aware, assertive, responsive, guiding
Decision-making	Does it on own	Delays or follows custom	Compromises; seeks happy medium	Strategically involves others; seeks optimal decision
Motivating	Negative reinforcement	Neither negative nor positive reinforcement	Indiscriminate positive reinforcement	Appropriate positive and negative reinforcement
Disagreement	Suppresses	Avoids	Smoothes over	Confronts and resolves
Communications	One-way	No-way	Part-way	Two-way

Figure 3.2   Sales management styles

Source: V. R. Buzzotta, R. E. Lefton, Manuel Sherberg, from copyrighted publication of Psychological Associates Inc., St. Louis, Mo., which may not be reproduced without express permission of their UK representatives P.S.I. International, Arundel, West Sussex, England.

Action-centred leadership

The well-known Action-centred Leadership (ACL) approach balances management style across the three Sales Management jobs:

- Achieve the task.
- Build the team.
- Satisfy individuals.

Key actions	Task	Team	Individual
Define objectives	Identify task and constraint	Involve team Share commitment	Clarify objective Gain acceptance
Plan	Establish priorities Check resources Decide set standards	Consult Encourage ideas and actions Develop suggestions structure	Assess skills Set targets Delegate
Brief	Brief the team Check understanding	Answer questions Obtain feedback	Listen Enthuse
Support Monitor	Report progress Maintain standards Discipline	Co-ordinate Reconcile conflict	Advise Assist/reassure Recognise effort Counsel
Evaluate	Summarise progress Review objectives Replan if necessary	Recognise success Learn from failure	Assess performance Appraise Guide and train

Figure 3.3

Source: John Adair, *Training for Leadership*, Gower Press, 1968

Many Sales Managers are too task-driven at the expense of team and individual needs, leading to demotivation.

Personality

In trying to find the right management style for the sales force (both collectively and individually), it is important to understand both your own personality and that of each team member.

Many 'personality conflicts' are caused by lack of understanding by the Sales Manager. It is necessary to understand why you get on well with some team members, but not so well with others. While you cannot change your personality (usually established in childhood), you can change your behaviour to modify its impact on others.

There are many personality profiles available, usually questionnaire-based (of which the Myers-Briggs profile is very much used world-wide).

Whatever personality profile is taken, a score and description will be provided on such aspects as:

- extraversion/introversion;

- sensing/intuition;

- thinking/feeling;

- judgement/perception (Myers–Briggs categories).

Combinations of characteristics will then produce a 'personality type', eg:

- traditionalist/judicial;

- troubleshooter/negotiator;

- visionary;

- catalyst.

Myers-Briggs, for example, produces 16 personality types and Belbin produces nine types for analysis in team roles.

Whatever profile is used, your personality profile wil enable you to understand (for you and your team):

- core values;

- strengths/weaknesses;

- normal ways of dealing with colleagues;

- reinforcement patterns;

- personality matches/conflicts;

- value to your company.

Knowledge of personality can at least help the Sales Manager to be sensitive to others and act accordingly, while ignorance of personality can only lead to crude stereotyped behaviour not based on perception.

Leadership

The combination of strong motivational skills and appropriate management styles produces what all successful Sales Managers possesss – leadership.

In modern sales forces, successful leaders will possess powerful skills in such areas as:

- individual/team involvement
- ownership
- empowerment
- teamwork
- communications

- freedom
- people development
- democracy
- innovation

This will produce a people-orientated, flattened structure with maximum team contributions, not an impersonal, hierarchical 'tell' culture, which is still endemic in many companies and is generally inappropriate for successful sales management.

There are many leadership profiles available to check your style of management, of which one of the most significant is LEAD (Hersey and Blanchard). This relates leadership style to the situation faced, measured in terms of "telling", "selling", "participating" or "delegating".

A recent study shows that learnt **emotional competencies**, such as persuasion, assertiveness, team leadership, political awareness, self-confidence, achievement, drive and, empathy produce star management performers. (Source: Working with Emotional Intelligence, Daniel Goleman, Bloomsbury).

Self-Appraisal for Sales Managers

Sales Manager Questionnaire	True	False
1 My staff respect me rather than fear me	☐	☐
2 I let my staff manage themselves to the maximum extent possible	☐	☐
3 I understand the personal needs of my staff	☐	☐
4 I treat all people alike and avoid playing favourites	☐	☐
5 I continually encourage suggestions and allow my staff to get involved in the planning of goals and objectives	☐	☐
6 I motivate my staff to give their best effort	☐	☐
7 I treat or motivate each person in the team in the same way	☐	☐
8 I tend to tell my subordinates what to do	☐	☐
9 I take a development attitude towards all staff	☐	☐
10 I understand the training needs of my staff and seek to continually develop their skills and achievements	☐	☐
11 I appraise performance regularly and allow feedback to be given to my staff and they to me	☐	☐
12 I believe that achievement and recognition are the best motivators	☐	☐
13 I set and agree many types of goals with my team and with each individual	☐	☐
14 I really care about staff	☐	☐
15 My attitude is totally positive	☐	☐
16 I consult with the team before deciding	☐	☐
17 I am too busy to try and develop myself for the good of the team	☐	☐
18 My job/role in the team is totally clear	☐	☐
19 I reward my staff for their results only – but recognise their efforts and encourage them to improve and for them to be winners	☐	☐
20 I am willing to take difficult decisions but consider the feelings of the staff	☐	☐
21 I understand the objectives of the team	☐	☐
22 I know the mission statements for our team	☐	☐
23 I understand the structure of our team	☐	☐
24 I understand the job roles within the structure	☐	☐
25 I understand fully my role and responsibilities within our team	☐	☐

Self-Appraisal for Sales Managers

Sales Force Questionnaire	True	False
1 I respect my boss rather than fear him/her	☐	☐
2 He/She lets me manage myself to the maximum extent possible	☐	☐
3 He/She understands my personal needs	☐	☐
4 He/She treats all people alike and avoids playing favourites	☐	☐
5 He/She continually encourages suggestions and allows me to get involved in the planning of goals and objectives	☐	☐
6 He/She motivates me to give my best effort	☐	☐
7 He/She treats or motivates each person in the team in the same way	☐	☐
8 He/She tends to tell his subordinates what to do	☐	☐
9 He/She takes a development attitude towards all staff	☐	☐
10 He/She understands my training needs and seeks to continually develop my skills and achievements	☐	☐
11 He/She appraises performance regularly and allows feedback to be given to me and received from me	☐	☐
12 I believe that achievement and recognition are the best motivators	☐	☐
13 He/She sets and agreed many types of goals with my team and with each individual	☐	☐
14 He/She really cares about staff	☐	☐
15 His/Her attitude to the job is totally positive	☐	☐
16 He/She consults with the team before deciding	☐	☐
17 He/She is too busy to try and develop him/herself for the good of the team	☐	☐
18 My job/role in the team is totally clear	☐	☐
19 He/She rewards me for my results only – but recognises my efforts and encourages me to improve and for me to be a winner	☐	☐
20 He/She is willing to take difficult decisions but considers the feelings of the staff	☐	☐
21 I understand the objectives of the team	☐	☐
22 I know the mission statements for our team	☐	☐
23 I understand the structure of our team	☐	☐
24 I understand the job roles within the structure	☐	☐
25 I understand fully my role and responsibilities within our team	☐	☐

CHECKPOINTS

- How would you describe your personality and style of management?

- How can you adapt your personality and style of management to the needs of your salesforce?

- How can you improve your team-working skills?

CHAPTER FOUR

Standards of performance

We have dealt so far with the need to:

- spend more time with the sales force;
- understand what motivates and demotivates, and treat motivation actively;
- understand the nature of Company culture and personality, and work towards a motivational management style.

These are core values and behaviours of successful Sales Managers. We must now begin to look at processes and actions which will produce successful sales teams, beginning with the establishment of clear, motivational standards of performance.

Sales task clarity – a key to better performance

Recent studies have identified that sales task clarity has a greater impact on the motivation of field salespeople than ego-drive or compensation method. Sales task clarity can also reinforce the effects of good recruitment and selection because it can make recruits with high ego-drive work harder and better. It can also reinforce a performance-orientated compensation system, but an imprecise task can prevent even the most clever system from working well.

Some sales tasks by their nature are less distinct than others, for example:

(a) A drug representative calling on a doctor to suggest prescribing a particular medicine:

- receives delayed feedback;
- needs a later prescription audit for that product and competing ones to discover whether a sale was even made.

(b) Selling electricity-generating equipment:

- the sale takes months or years and involves many people.

Motivation and performance

Motivation is difficult to define and hard to measure. Multiple measures of sales force motivation are necessary to determine the impact of sales task clarity. These are:

- Sales performance against objectives.
- Supervisor's performance evaluation.
- Amount of time worked per week.
- Strength of salesperson's belief that effort would be rewarded.

In a sample study, salespeople in businesses where the sales task was clear scored 30-60 percent higher on motivation measures than those where it wasn't. All the businesses studied looked for recruits with a strong need to achieve and with big ego drives, so the differences in motivation evidently came from differences in sales task clarity, not recruitment and selection practices.

Type of pay plan – incentive versus straight salary – also had less impact than the clarity of the task. Task clarity was 50 per cent more important in determining motivation than personality, and nearly three times as important as type of pay plan. It therefore seems clear that clarity of task is the most important element in salesperson motivation.

When the elements of the job were indistinct, the salespeople did not know where they stood and could not get reinforcement from news of their performance. One sales representative said, 'Selling in this industry is like living in a dream. Getting ahead is a matter of luck and politics. It's discouraging.'

Salespeople also tend to stay longer in companies with better sales task clarity than others. A district Sales Manager of one of the latter commented, 'Turnover is a real problem. We hire aggressive young trainees and fire them up with training. When they get out on the street, however, frustration becomes a problem. These people want to know how they are doing and how competitive they are. Many of the reps who quit are uncomfortable with our type of selling.'

Job standards

A key part of clarity is the definition of job standards. The process should contain the following elements:

1 Write down all the key tasks of the sales force.

2 Check that all these tasks are included in the job description (if not, *update* it).

3 Group the tasks into a logical sales sequence against each of which you can describe a Standard of Performance in qualitative terms.

4 Develop quantitative standards and ratios for key results areas.

The following example (Fig. 4.1) from fast-moving consumer goods shows very clear standards and can be recommended as a model guide on publishing clear standards to any company. The sales force can be involved in establishing the standards and the guide can be produced quickly and updated easily. It is particularly helpful for new members of the sales team.

It is especially important to update the standards of performance to reflect job role changes. In the example given, changes in the growth of major customers and ways of selling would make many of the standards inappropriate for today's sales force. The important principle is always to publish clear, up-to-date standards of performance.

Standards of Performance

(Business Results Guide)

TERRITORY SALES REPRESENTATIVE

Elements of my job vital for success are:

* *Sell across the range of products and introduce new lines*
* *Sell promotion deals*
* *Maintain optimum stock cover*
* *Increase shelf space*
* *Negotiate second sitings on shelf or shop floor and better fixture positions*

KEY ELEMENTS	STEP	AREA	STANDARD OF PERFORMANCE
Sell across the range of products & introduce new lines	1. Planning & Preparation	The day	Has everything needed to achieve the day's business plans; emphasise personal appearance & general turnout; car arrangements, equipment, samples and other materials. Plans to achieve an economic journey and satisfy calls-per-day targets.
		The call	Completes call preparation the evening prior to the call & reviews it immediately before each call.
		Product range	Plans to achieve stocking of all authorised products in each call, using knowledge of each customer's stocking lists, merchandising policy & current support information.
		Information sources	Has available all up-to-date information needed for effective call planning, particularly in respect of: the Market: the trade; current promotional activity; Action priorities; targeting requirements; trade dealing policy; product distribution arrangements.
		Call objectives	Plans objectives in line with the Company's priorities, taking into account: National & VIP account activity, marketing priorities, trade funds, frequency/volume requirements & tactical priorities. Sets personal objectives for each call based on problems/opportunities within the outlet.
SELL PROMO-TIONAL DEALS		Promotions	Aims promotional plans at achieving calculated quantities in line with volume targets. Ensures correct use of all Company resources, particularly TD, TIF & merchandisers (if appropriate).
	2. Account	Credit control	Knows the account situation for each call & maintains credit within defined limits.
		Collection	Collects accounts according to the laid-down procedures & implements stops when/where appropriate.

Figure 4.1   Guide to standards of performance

Maintain optimum stock cover	3. Store/stock check	Normal servicing	Carries out normal servicing procedures in each call with objective of correcting any deficiencies to standard through store management, merchandiser or personal action. Checks that the assumptions within Tactical Plan are correct in respect of: complete range distribution v. listing; shelf space allocated is, at least, in line with market share variety split; shelf position matches plans; assess level of stock on shelf & replacement quantity; ensure products are first in traffic flow; that off-shelf displays are adequate to support promotions; that products are clearly and correctly priced and are competitive; that (where applicable) the merchandiser's performance is in line with objectives. Identifies new opportunities resulting from any in-store changes. Investigates problem areas in order to find solutions which meet the needs of the buyer and his business.
		Stock check	Makes maximum use of in-store shelf & display space in bringing stock forward. Count all remaining back stock, identify spoiled or out-of-date stock, and ensure stock rotation operates. Be familiar with each store's stock control system.
		Proposed order	Carries out the correct series of calculations in order to arrive at an adequate stock holding level for non-promotional lines, for each outlet. Determines the original promotional quantity objectives in the light of the stock situation.
		Staff motivation	Obtains the co-operation of store staff in the low skilled aspects of merchandising such as routine pricing, shelf filling, box arranging, stock rotation. Identifies section responsibility of key warehouse staff. Utilise staff assistance in proposals to the buyer.
	4. Presentation	Opening the sale	Makes an identifiable effort to gain the buyer's initial attention & interest by careful use of the right opening words & skilful use of selling tools.
		Presentation	Makes a planned, clearly defined presentation in support of objectives, achieving a positive reaction from the buyer. Makes skilful use of the appropriate selling tools. Provides a precise explanation of each relevant product feature & converts it into a benefit to the buyer.
		Handling objections	Responds to, and deals with, objections appropriately & convincingly, leaving the buyer satisfied. Prepares the presentation sufficiently to avoid/anticipate normal objections.
	5. Close	Closing the sale	Closes at the peak of the buyer's interest, using an appropriate close to secure agreement to the 3 main objectives of stock and order, promotional quantities & merchandising aims.

Figure 4.1 Continued

Increase shelf space	**6. Merchandising**	Shelf space	Plans to achieve optimum shelf space over and above the minimum level of current brand shares.
			Plans should indicate knowledge of each account's current policy; contact with Merchandising & Store Management; familiarity with current market information; knowledge of throughput/return per linear foot for Company and the competition; most appropriate use of support material.
		Shelf merchandising	Makes every effort to ensure that, on leaving the store, our brands are prominent, at the front of the traffic flow, accessible & correctly priced.
Negotiate second sitings on shelf or shop floor & better fixture positions		Display space	Ensures that display plans achieve maximum impact for Company products, taking into consideration: each store's policy on promotional displays & merchandising material; the relationship between display costs & promotional return long-term product growth objectives; merchandising resources.
		Multi-sites	Gets multi-sites prominently positioned in store where extra purchasing opportunities exist.
		Feature merchandising	Position displays in the best available site.
	Administration	Territory & daily completion	Ensures that overall territory & daily administration is complete & meets postal deadlines.
	Self appraisal	Evaluation	After each call evaluates achievement against objectives set. Communicates good selling ideas.
		Self analysis	Isolate areas of weakness against performance standards for special attention.
	Selling tools	Customer record book	Uses the C.R.B. to plan all aspects of the call.
		Stock & order sheet	Uses the S.O.S. to plan & justify order size & overcome objections.
		Brand talk	Familiar with all key points/features of every brand and is able to translate them into benefits to the buyer.
		Sample	Kept in good condition, handled to the best effect and where appropriate handed to the customer.
		Organiser	Uses Organiser to emphasise the key points of the presentation, and makes own inserts as necessary.

Figure 4.1   Continued

Figure 4.2 relates standards of performance to Key Results Areas and Controls and Monitors for evaluating results of behaviours.

Key Result Areas	Minimum Standards of Performance	Controls and Monitors
achievement of sales targets	90% of budget over 3 month period	3 month team review
open new accounts	minimum of 4 per month	monthly review
adequate call rate	minimum average call rate of 7.5 calls per day	daily call report and monthly review
site visits	familiar with all large and medium sized sites in area	daily call reports and area survey forms
sales methods	knowledge of the sales process and required level of skill: 1. drive 2. empathy 3. selling techniques 4. work organisation & planning 5. use of product knowledge	field appraisal monthly summary from sales management annual appraisal
adequate route planning	have a formulated workable system to avoid waste of time and travel costs	daily call reports and petrol expense call forms
knowledge of competitors (pricing and activity)	collate information for sales meetings	verbal report from each representative at sales meetings as and when required. Also submit competitors' price lists as required
flexibility to participate in sales drives on other areas including sales blitzes	individual's performance against other team members and team average result	analysis of written report of results
involvement in company/ branch/region promotions and events	in accordance with reasonable company requests	ongoing

Figure 4.2   Relating Standards of Performance to Key Result Areas and Controls and Monitors

Note: This is an example of some standards of performance, not the complete job

Competences

In some industries, particularly financial services, the subject of job standards for the sales force has been taken to very precise levels. The object is to 'certificate' all sales staff so that selling is to defined standards (in financial services, described as 'best advice').

Apart from the regulatory requirements of Competences, the principle of job clarity improvement can apply to all sales forces although not necessarily in such a sophisticated way. It is worth testing the idea of Competences on the sales force and involving them in producing the Levels and Competence categories.

The Competence model includes the following elements:

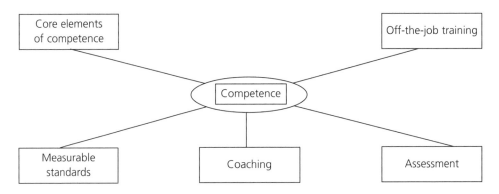

Core elements of competence

The Competence categories will be all the key elements of the Standards of Performance guide (see Fig. 4.1 above). Each one will be broken down into written detail, for each level of sales person, eg: Trainee (new); Level 1 (the average salesperson); Level 2 (advanced salesperson).

Example

Competence example (one element only of the job)

Skills

Sales:

Closing the sale:
This is so that sales are maximised by asking for the business at the appropriate time.

What you will be assessed on

1. Recognising buying signals.

2. Using positive and descriptive language to help the customer to buy.

3. Being able to find different ways to ask for the business.

4. Being able to cope with rejection.

5. Completing sale forms correctly.

6. Asking for referrals.

How you will be assessed

1. Observation.

2. Discussion.

3. Role play.

Measurable standards/guidelines

1. At least 1.5 sales per week.

2. 80 per cent second appointment rate.

3. 80 per cent asking for commitment rate.

4. Asks for referrals on 50 per cent of occasions.

Off-the-job training

This will be given to each level of salesperson as a foundation for on-the-job performance.

Measurable standards

It is desirable to agree measurable standards at each level (as in the example) in order to avoid subjective assessment of competence achievement by different Sales Managers. Guidelines can be created for behavioural standards at, for example, 4 levels – Ineffective; Needs Developing; Effective; Desired.

Coaching

In order to help each salesperson to achieve job Competences, Sales Managers must be skilled coaches – often the Achilles' heel of many sales forces (see Chapter 8).

Assessment

This will usually be by an agreed pattern of field observations, tests (for product knowledge), discussion and role plays.

Any Competences scheme needs piloting to ensure it is motivational and practical. There could be, for example, 40 or 50 Competences to be assessed and recorded across the two or three levels of the sales force – a significant workload for Field Sales Managers. Most salespeople like the motivational elements of Competences (it delivers all the Herzberg motivators – achievement, recognition, work itself, responsibility, advancement and personal growth), but the approach must be practical and workable to be effective.

Ways to enhance sales task clarity

1. Deployment

Often salespeople are assigned territories with only geographic boundaries and given little more than 'hunting licences'. But important parts of task clarity are a limitation on the number of accounts for which each person has responsibility and specification of goals for each of these target accounts.

Few salespeople can regularly handle more than about 50 accounts in a situation in which a real sales effort, instead of a cursory presentation effort, is necessary. Yet some companies assign several hundred accounts to each salesperson or give them all the accounts in a geographic area. Doing so can only lead to frustration as the salespeople realise they have no set priorities and are powerless to control their performance.

The more specific the account coverage, the better it is; for example, better to list the accounts for each person. If necessary, a part of the defined task can be the salesperson's responsibility to add to the list a number of qualified prospects. The important thing is that salespeople understand which accounts they are responsible for and will be judged by.

2. Account management

Salespeople must have clear objectives to achieve for each account – total sales objectives, activity objectives, sales goals by product type (if relevant), etc. The more measurable the goals/objectives, the clearer the task definition and the greater the motivation. Objectives can, of course, go beyond sales to include matters such as presentations, proposals and penetration to specified members of the buying organisation. But the objectives must be attainable. It can be extremely demotivational to include in a person's objectives, tasks over which he or she has little or no control; frustration and anxiety are the result.

3. Information systems

The information system gives the connection between actual and reported performance; a poor information system will destroy the salesperson's perception of a direct relationship between effort and results.

The information system, more than any other tool, determines the timeliness and accuracy of feedback which is vital to task clarity. Random factors can ruin the quality of performance feedback. Delay in the information flow reduces the salespeople's ability to remember their effort (at both the intellectual and emotional level) and to relate it to reported results.

4. Field sales management

To ensure task clarity for each salesperson, the Manager can use a variety of management mechanisms and processes. Most of these centre on the goal-setting, feedback, coaching, and appraisal cycle. They include management by objectives, performance appraisal, and monthly reviews. But they require the commitment of the manager responsible, beginning with deployment and account planning. The manager tailors the task to the particular salesperson, sales territory and accounts. Even more important from a motivational viewpoint is ensuring, through a dialogue with the salesperson, that he or she understands and accepts the task as laid out; often, the task of clarifying the sales task will test the cleverness and ingenuity of any Sales Manager.

At the other end of the cycle – appraisal – the Manager helps the salesperson to interpret the results and relate them to the defined task and the salesperson's effort. So, the Manager helps to clarify and amplify the definition of the task and the measurement of results.

Naturally, an organisation's Sales Managers must understand their task and be trained to accomplish it. But no Sales Manager, regardless of ability or training, can work effectively with a poor information or compensation system that rewards people haphazardly instead of for clearly defined results.[1]

[1]Reprinted by permission of *Harvard Business Review*. 'Ideas for action: make the sales task clear', Benson P. Shapiro and Stephen X. Doyle, Vol 61 No. 6 (Nov/Dec 1983). Copyright © 1983 by the President and Fellows of Harvard College; all rights reserved.

Summary of Possible Actions to Enhance Sales Task Clarity

1. **Deployment**
   - Limitations on numbers of accounts held to help focus sales activities
   - Goals for target accounts
   - Call frequencies established for each account
   - Prospect accounts allocated by sales manager

2. **Account Management**
   - Clear objectives set by Account
   - Broken down targets by product/customer size
   - Need to write account plans for larger customers
   - Activity targets set eg levels of contact with customer

3. **Information System**
   - Forms link between targets, activities and results
   - Provides data to re-form action plans
   - Accuracy necessary so sales person believes data provided
   - Speed of provision of information guides behaviour
   - Presentation style helps clarity of understanding

4. **Field Training**
   - Attitude, skill and knowledge measurement helps to give clarity of behaviour understanding
   - Standards need to be set for all parts of the selling job, eg asking questions, selling benefits.
   - Measurable clear standards can be set (eg below standards; meets standard; exceeds standard; exceptional)
   - Regular field coaching gives continuous feedback.

Weighting job elements

An excellent way to promote job clarity and awareness of standards of performance is to produce a weighted average of four key job areas:

1 Results

2 Knowledge

3 Skills

4 Attitudes.

The objective is to show to the sales force how important achieving results is in relation to the abilities which lead to results.

An example would be:

	'Hard sell' company	'Soft sell' company
Results	65%	15%
Knowledge	15%	25%
Skill	10%	40%
Attitude	10%	20%
Total	100%	100%

The 'Hard Sell' company is saying to the sales force that it values results much more highly than the methods and qualities of selling by which they are achieved; while the 'Soft Sell' company values the acquisition of knowledge, skills and attitude much more highly, so customers are given high quality sales representation.

This weighted average job clarity has applications in a number of sales management areas, as we shall see in later chapters:

- Recruitment criteria
- Motivation emphasis
- Pay (via 'points for achievement' systems)
- Coaching (field assessment)
- Job priorities

- Job promotion criteria
- Planning/control.

The sales force needs to know not only what job aspects are important and to what standards, but what weighting in importance does each aspect have. Such a weighted average shows that not all parts of the selling job are of equal importance – a very useful concept to apply in guiding sales management priorities and emphasis.

Quantitative standards

Qualitative standards, both in terms of job clarity and relative importance, are vital to successful sales management.

Quantitative standards provide the measurable clarity which is the basis of good motivation and control in sales management.

A relatively small number of Key Results Areas should be established, then individual and team targets should be agreed for each Standard.

Each Company can then establish its own key results areas, relating input (effort) to output (result).

The following 12 key ratios would form the basis of an excellent motivation and control system in most sales forces:

12 KEY RATIOS	Demonstrates
1 Orders per call (strikerate)	converting opportunities
2 Average order size	high value selling
3 Prospects/enquiries/proposals to sales	activity productivity
4 Approaches to appointments	activity levels
5 Appointments to proposals	assertiveness
6 Major accounts to total sales	mix of customers
7 Number of lines per order	range selling
8 Sales per hour of selling time	time effectiveness
9 Sales to cost ratio	profit focus
10 Call rate per account	service levels
11 New accounts to existing accounts	prospecting skill
12 Sales to market potential ratio	market focus

These quantitative standards help the salesperson to evaluate his or her own performance to see why sales occur (or do not). They can form the basis of self-targeting (achievement motivation), and help the Sales Manager to understand why some of the team perform better than others. Measuring results only (volume of sales, value of sales, profit) will not help to analyse why sales occur.

Many sales forces have no regular targeting and analysis of such ratios (many more than those given above could be established). More time is given to this subject in Chapter 5, Planning and control.

CHECKPOINTS

- What Standards of Performance do you have in place now?
- How clear are these standards?
- How can you create more clarity by redifining the sales force standards of performance?

CHAPTER FIVE

Planning and control

Many Sales Managers pay too little attention to the motivational benefits of a good Sales Planning and Control System. They often treat this aspect of sales management as mechanical and 'boring', and as a result produce a demotivational process.

Planning is an attitude of mind as well as a process, designed to:

(a) Predict the future trends affecting the business.

(b) Influence what we should be trying to achieve.

(c) Describe how we plan to achieve our objectives.

(d) Feed-back how we are doing against Plan.

(e) Act, not just react.

(f) Focus on activities to achieve results.

The major *problems* of sales planning are:

1 Budgets only, not Plans (ie 'What', not 'How').

2 Lack of sales force involvement and ownership in Planning.

3 Poor sales analysis.

4 Lack of a 'vision' and a sales strategy from Management.

5 Plans in the head only, not written or communicated.

6 Lack of common plan formats.

7 Too little time to plan.

8 Poor information on results against plans.

t know where you're going, any road will take you there.'

description of the three types of Company aptly describes variations in ills:

1 Those Companies who make things happen (Act).

2 Those Companies who watch things happen (React).

3 Those Companies who wonder what happened (Bankrupt!).

The planning process – Top-down v. Bottom-up

Top down

A key issue in successful sales management is to ensure the target-setting and planning system is realistic, fair and motivational. This is particularly important if bonus pay or commission is a high part of total remuneration. Nothing demotivates a salesperson more than to work hard to achieve unrealistic targets, while a colleague in another territory achieves success and rewards because of perceived 'easy' targets, or a high luck factor.

This is a very complex subject, going all the way back to the Company's sales and profit goals at Board level. It is often a very political subject, involving ego and status at all levels.

The dangers of a typical 'Top-down' target-setting system are:

(a) Unrealistically high targets against territory potential in some areas.

(b) Unrealistically low targets in areas where potential is high.

(c) 'Switching off' if the target is seen to be unrealistic.

(d) Higher staff turnover rates.

(e) Low morale due to lack of involvement and ownership of targets.

Overall sales performance can be seriously impaired, as low achievers against top-down targets may give up, while high achievers may coast once the target is achieved. Companies try to deal with this problem by a variety of allocation methods, eg:

(i) Equal targets for everyone.

(ii) Targets allocated by territory population size.

(iii) Targets allocated by buying power index methods.

(iv) Targets allocated by market size estimates.

(v) Targets allocated by previous sales performance.

Each method has strengths and weaknesses for each company, but does not solve the fundamental problem of lack of involvement and ownership of targets by the sales force.

Bottom up

Bottom-up targeting has many advantages over top-down methods, but also requires longer time periods for planning and more skills of forecasting.

If the Company culture is conducive to involving staff in decision-making (as recommended as a constant theme in this book), then bottom-up can work effectively as follows:

Bottom–up targeting

National sales goals
(set by Board)

Discussion/negotiation → Marketing plans/information

Regional sales goals
(1st estimate, allocation)

Discussion/negotiation

Territory forecasts
(individual bids)

Agreed targets (individual)

Sales plans (individual)

The process works as follows:

1 The Board sets national sales goals, as part of the corporate plan, informed by marketing plans/information.

2 The National Sales Manager allocates the national sales goals to regions, but only as a first estimate, subject to discussion/negotiation.

3 The Regional Managers asks for 'bids' from the sales force for individual shares of the regional targets.

4 The sales force bids, based on their own assessment of territory potential, informed by marketing plans (eg new products, de-listings, promotion, advertising, product priorities).

5 These bids are discussed/negotiated with Regional Managers.

6 Once agreed, the targets are supported by individual sales plans – how the targets will be achieved.

If the Company culture is right for this process, national and regional targets will sometimes be exceeded by individual bids (achievement motivation, involvement). If not, negotiation will usually produce amicable and fair targets. At least everyone will have been involved in the process and motivation will be maximised.

FEATURES OF TOP-DOWN AND BOTTOM-UP PLANNING

	TOP-DOWN	BOTTOM-UP
Targets	Allocated	Bid
Market knowledge	Low	High
Forecasting skill	Low	High
Resource control	Fixed	Variable
Action plans	Optional	Essential
Timing	Late	Early
Responsibility	Low	High
Involvement	Low	High
Motivation	Low	High
Market-based	No	Yes
Emphasis	Budgets	Planning
Sales management	Results	Activities

Sales plans

The sales planning process, like marketing planning, has five stages:

1 Where are we now? (Analysis)

2 Where are we heading? (Forecasting)

3 Where do we want to be? (Objectives)

4 How will we get there? (Sales Plans)

5 How will we know we are getting there? (Control)

In diagram form, this can be expressed as shown in Fig. 5.1:

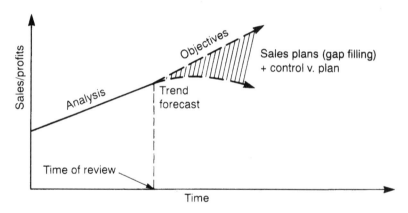

Figure 5.1   The importance of sales plans in relation to trends and objectives

The sales plans need to fill the gap between the Trend line (where we will be if we continue doing as we are doing now) and the Objectives line (where we would like to be).

The Trend line means that a large part of any sales target will be achieved by no new actions, ie existing customers and random effects will produce significant Trend business - perhaps 75 per cent of the annual target.

The Objective line and sales plans (gap-filling) need to be in harmony, ie testing objectives, but achievable by defined sales plans.

Objectives that bear no relation to trends of sales or sales plans are a recipe for disaster. If sales trends are down, and activities are inadequate, how can ambitious sales objectives be achieved? Part of this air of unreality goes back to a lack of bottom-up planning, and a wish that the self-fulfilling prophecy will be achieved. Wishes rarely produce sales results.

Sales plan format

1 Information analysis

- Total market trends

- Product trends

- Sector trends

- Customer trends

- Sales analysis v. market (market share)

- Competitive activity

- Sales team analysis

- Control reports analysis

- Organisation analysis

- SWOTs (strengths/weaknesses/opportunities/threats)

2 Volume/share/profit objectives

(£, units, %), by Market/Customers

3 Major strategies and actions

- Market developement

- Product emphasis

- Key customer plans

- Organisation

- Selling methods (eg telesales v. personal calling)

- Call frequencies

- Recruitment

- Training

- Control reports/methods

- Pricing/discounts

- Promotions

4 **Expenditure budget**

5 **Timetable of events**

Each member of the sales team needs an annual sales plan. The Sales Manager writes down the 'vision' and the main methods of achievement. Typically, for a Regional Sales Manager, this would be 7-10 pages in length. It would be distributed and regularly reviewed each month during the year – not put in the drawer and forgotten about, as is often the case!

Each sales team member writes a short plan of how the targets they have been involved in setting up will be achieved. This will be the basis of achievement orientation and regular review against individual plans – the best way to motivate performance.

Sales Plans work best if they have the following features:

- Common formats, so Managers and sales team members address the same issues.

- Analysis proformas, for ease of completion (an example is given below in Fig. 5.2).

- Short and to the point.

- Able to be measured in the Control System.

- Flexibility, so they can be changed if necessary.

- Creative, with enough activity to fill the sales/profit gap.

- Focus, so that the sales force concentrates on the best customer and product profit opportunities (this can be summarised by the phrase 'Fish where the fish are fish in the right ponds, make bigger catches and don't lose the fish that are caught').

Sales analysis – product/market matrix

	Market 1	Market 2	Market 3	Product Trend	Total
Product 1	100 / 60	2000 / 80	400 / 150	Increasing 33% p.a.	2500 / 290
Product 2	500 / 30	1000 / 100	2000 / 100	Decreasing 7% p.a.	3500 / 230
Product 3	1200 / 100	2400 / 200	1600 / 40	Increasing 2% p.a.	5200 / 340
Market Trend	Static	Growing 14% p.a.	Increasing 3% p.a.		
Total	1800 / 190	5400 / 380	4000 / 290		11200 / 860

P = Potential purchasers, i.e. market size
A = Actual purchases from us

Figure 5.2   In this example, **Market 2, Product 1** should be a target for sales growth, as it combines Market Growth (+14% pa) with Product Growth (+33%), and the Company has a low market share (80/2000, or 4%, compared with overall market share of 860/11,200, or 7.7%).

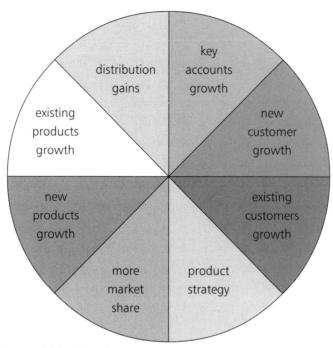

Figure 5.3   Sources of Sales Growth

10 Step decision making model

	Steps	Check	Example
1	Setting objectives	Are they specific and quantitative?	To increase sales revenue in west region by 10 per cent in next six months compared with same period last year. To increase customers to 1000. To hold sales costs at same level as last year.
2	Evaluating the objectives	Do they conflict with other goals?	Production is available, also promotional help.
3	Collecting the information	Have the questions to be answered been clearly defined?	Need last year's sales broken down by customer, product and salesperson. Also market research data on potential available and competitive activity.

4	Analysing the information	Is it known what is being searched for?	Specific questions to be answered include: Can current customers buy more? How many prospects are there? What is current sales force call rate? What is order/call ratio?
5	Developing alternatives	Have all alternatives been listed?	(Assuming above work done) a) Increase call frequency on customers b) Increase prospecting rate c) Improve selling skills by training
6	Choosing the 'best' alternative	Have all alternatives been evaluated in terms of cost, time, risk and resources?	a) Cost increase because need more staff. Delay in recruiting. Risk in taking on more new staff. Personnel department resources involved. b) No cost – can do with existing sales force. Some time to reorganise. Low risk. Low resources. c) Cost of training. Time for training. Experience elsewhere shows training effective, therefore risk low. No resources, can use consultants. Choose c) as likely to be most effective, though not cheapest.
7	Communicating the decision	Have the right people been told the appropriate information by the appropriate methods?	Advise marketing director by memorandum. Brief sales force at meeting. Give terms of reference to consultants at meeting.
8	Measuring the decision	What will be measured; how and when?	Best yardsticks of increased effectiveness are order to call ratio and average order size. Monitor now before action starts.
9	Implementing the decision	Have specific tasks been allocated with specific timings?	Run training programme. Revise sales targets. Concentrate on lists of customers with further potential.
10	Evaluating the decision	Has the decision been evaluated against the objectives?	Appraisal for training programme. Actuals against targets on monthly basis.

Sales control

Once the correct motivational planning system is in place, the Sales Manager can now carry out day-to-day control of sales performance, using agreed productivity ratios (see Chapter 4, Standards of performance).

The Control System should follow the selling process (Fig. 5.4), which exists in each Company, with information collected at each level.

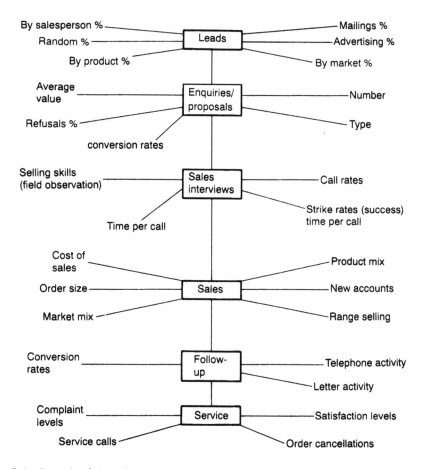

Figure 5.4   Example of the selling process

Managing with information

The basis of all Sales Management control (managing with information) is to recognise **key results areas**, and then to manage by analysing performance against **standards of performance**. Corrective action can then be taken quickly and focused on Key Results Areas.

Standards of performance can be expressed as **absolute numbers**.

> eg: 'to achieve ten calls per day average'

or as **ratios**:

> eg: 'to achieve 40 per cent conversion of proposals to orders'

or **qualitatively**:

> eg: 'To sell a balanced range of products'.

As standards are achieved they can be re-set and agreed with the sales force – a constant 'flag planting' process, aimed at keeping performance always in the mind's attention.

1. Analysis of information

As information is produced monthly and cumulatively, the Manager is looking for **warning lights** which he or she can identify and then investigate to find **causes** of performance.

Warning lights could be:

- Declining absolute sales levels.
- Falling average sales per district.
- Fall in league position.
- Product sales problems.
- Shortfall of sales against plan.
- Increasing trend of decline (sudden or long-term?).
- Position against district averages.
- Fall in average order sizes (£).
- Fall in numbers of orders.
- Cancelled order trends.

These warning lights do not in themselves suggest problems, because a short-term decline may not be significant. Also, unless information is related to a performance standard, few conclusions can be drawn.

2. Setting standards of performance

In some cases the standard is obvious, eg shortfall against a sales plan figure. In others, a reported figure should be related to a **standard** set, agreed by the Manager with the team.

As an example, one district may be low on sales of a certain product, but if its market potential for this product is less than other districts, the low sales figure is not significant. It is significant if it has agreed a realistic product sales goal.

The basic management principle is to agree standards at all levels for every category of performance measure, so that management action is appropriate when a **variance** arises when comparing standard and result. This is called **management by exception**, ie acting only when unusual variances in performance arise.

3. Corrective action

This is the creative process whereby the Manager agrees with the team an improvement programme.

Action plans can be very **informal**, eg a telephone call and discussion of ideas, or **formal**, eg a three-month review meeting with full analysis of sales performance.

In action planning, it is always wise to *write down* the plan, as it focuses both Manager and team on the tasks and allows easy review of results achieved.

A common layout is:

Objective	Action	Timing
1		
2		
etc		

The cause of sales problems

Diagnosing the cause of sales problems is often an exhaustive process, eg:

1. Productivity causes

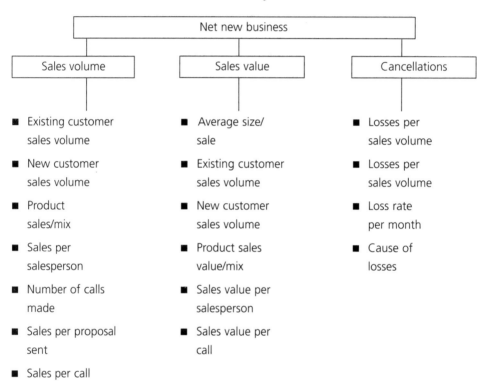

Call reports and direct data entry should be designed to collect information through reports, so these analyses can be carried out easily – not by excessive manual analysis, as is often the case. Automated sales activity reporting is now a key part of Customer Relationship Management, provided by many leading edge suppliers.

Graphs can be produced relating one productivity ratio to sales results, so the reasons for sales results can be closely analysed. Two examples are given below, in Figs 5.5 and 5.6.

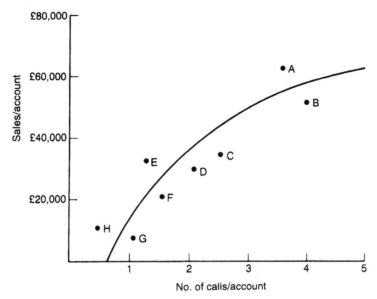

Figure 5.5   This graph shows a close relationship between calls per account and sales per account. If low performing sales personnel (eg H, G) can be motivated to increase their call rates for each account (perhaps reducing cold calling), it is likely sales per account would grow steadily. This is typical of high service markets.

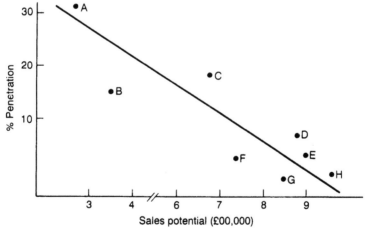

Figure 5.6   This graph shows five sales team members with high sales potential, but low territory penetration (less than 10 per cent customers to prospects ratio). Salesperson A has low sales potential, but converts over 30 per cent of prospects to customers. The implication is that territory sizes may be too large to allow proper call coverage. Smaller territories with better call rates should produce much higher penetration rates, and more sales personnel would probably be cost effective.

2. Management causes

- Motivation

- Training (levels of skill, knowledge, and attitude)

- Planning

- Promotion

- Organisation

- Incentives

- Recruitment

- Sales area coverage

- Service of customers

These causes can often only be identified from personal meetings and discussion with the Manager/salesperson concerned, as they have the relevant information to hand.

At these meetings, *style* of conduct is a key factor in motivating the team to improve performance.

Key aspects of style are:

- *Sell* ideas, don't tell
  (they must own the solutions).

- *Invite ideas*/solutions.

- *Praise* first, criticism second.

- *Ask* for goals, don't impose them.

- *Reprimand* constructively.

- *Listen*.

- Be *clear* what you mean.

- *Consult* before deciding.

- *Select words* carefully.

- *Enthusiasm*.

- *Record ideas* during and at end of meeting.

- *Summarise* periodically.

Remember
'People buy what **they want***'*
'People buy people first'

SUMMARY

Using management information effectively is a vital part of the management process:

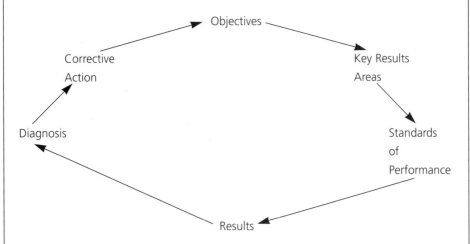

The effective Sales Manager:

- Knows what he or she wants to achieve.
- Communicates goals/vision to the team.
- Uses management information systematically and creatively.
- Motivates the team to take corrective action.
- Keeps seeking performance improvement.

CHECKPOINTS

- How can you improve the quality of sales plans?
- How can you set targets more motivationally?
- How can you use sales information better?

CHAPTER SIX

Organisation

All Sales Managers need to evaluate whether the organisation structure is right for the changes which have taken place over time, and for future needs.

The selling job

Any organisation review should list the current sales activities of the sales force, and decide if any activities could be re-allocated to other staff.

Current Sales Force Task	Alternative
1 Credit control	Sales administration department; Head Office credit control; Accountancy department
2 Merchandising	Dedicated merchandising staff (possibly part-time, lower cost)
3 Promotions	Marketing department
4 Large customer calling	Head Office national/regional account Managers
5 Small customer calling	Telesales; wholesaler servicing
6 Prospecting	New business sales force
7 Demonstration	Special demonstration team
8 After-sales service	Service team

Once tasks are reallocated, the job description for sales staff can be rewritten to provide job clarity.

Span of control

Sales Managers at each level need to assess whether the functions to be managed and the number of staff are allowing the management job to be done effectively (see Chapter 1).

Sales teams of six to eight people can be managed effectively in most situations, although wide geographical dispersion makes this harder. If all the sales team members are geographically close (eg based in a Sales Office), then up to 12 can be managed by one person although it is always best for motivational/coaching/counselling reasons to have a 1:6 ratio (or less) per team. Smaller teams also improve internal competitive motivation, help to develop managers more quickly, and give a career development track.

Organisation methods[1]

1. Geographical organisation

This is still the most common organisation structure of sales teams, benefiting from:

- Simplicity
- Proximity to customers
- Low travel expenses.

It works on the assumption that convenience and lower costs outweigh any disadvantages, eg lack of product range selling effort, or poor customer servicing.

A typical structure would be:

HEAD OF SALES

| Regional Sales Manager | Regional Sales Manager | Regional Sales Manager |

| Territory Sales Staff | Territory Sales Staff | Territory Sales Staff |

[1] Extracts in this Chapter are reproduced from *Sales Force Management in Europe*, 1986, the Economist Intelligence Unit.

Geographical sales organisation becomes inappropriate when:

(i) product lines proliferate, meaning very few lines are actually sold at each sales visit;

(ii) the product range becomes too complex technically for sales staff to understand all the features and benefits;

(iii) customer segments develop special servicing requirements which territory sales forces cannot fulfil;

(iv) product group or divisional Managers cannot get enough selling time for their special needs;

(v) the quality of field intelligence becomes too low due to lack of specialist knowledge.

As one European Sales Manager said:

'We are living in a world of segmented products and markets – and to get the best results, most firms will have to start segmenting their sales forces. But, believe me, this isn't an easy route to take . . .'

'The basic problem is costs: running a specialised sales force means high training costs, as well as higher salaries. It also leaves you much more vulnerable to sudden departures among sales people. But I personally feel that the opportunity costs you carry by employing an all-purpose sales force are just too great. A few years ago, most companies couldn't afford specialised sales forces. In the future, I suspect that very few companies will be able to afford generalists.'

2. Product organisation

As product lines proliferate and technology increases, many companies begin to separate the sales force into product groups, as follows:

The **advantages** of this approach are:

- Higher sales as a result of greater product knowledge.

- Improved margins due to emphasis on product benefits other than price.

- Greater customer satisfaction for each product group.

- Better feedback on customer needs.

The **disadvantages** are:

- Higher training costs.

- Lower call rates.

- Higher expense levels.

- Customer annoyance if too many visits from the same firm occur, with different sales staff.

- Administrative problems (sharing secretarial and administrative help).

3. Market organisation

Product organisation may not be appropriate when customer or market groups require special understanding and have very different needs. Increasingly organisation by industry or market segment may give companies a competitive edge. A typical structure would be as follows:

The **advantages** of this form of organisation are:

- Greater customer orientation and higher sales.

- Develops customer loyalty.

- Provides best type of intelligence from the field.

The **disadvantages** are:

- Very high costs (especially training).
- Increased market support expenditure (promotion, service, etc).
- Vulnerability to sales force defection.
- Needs high product knowledge to sell range in each segment.

4. Size of account organisation

Organisation by account size can be relevant to all sizes of company, but becomes critically important with company size.

It follows the 80:20 principle to its logical conclusion: 80 per cent of sales come from 20 per cent of customers, but the same 20 per cent may not account for 80 per cent of profits. A typical structure would be:

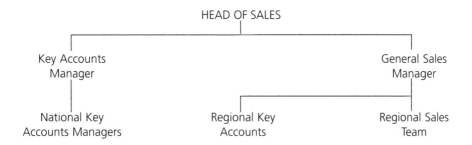

HEAD OF SALES

Key Accounts Manager — General Sales Manager

National Key Accounts Managers — Regional Key Accounts — Regional Sales Team

The main **advantages** of this form of organisation are:

- Gives maximum attention to the most important individual customers (profit impact of customer retention).
- Allows terms of business and servicing to reflect customer importance (Customer Relationship Management).
- Provides very accurate customer intelligence.
- Reduces need for territory sales staff, or their replacement with lower cost service staff.

- Facilitates decisions on smaller account servicing eg move to telesales, or delisting to wholesaler servicing.

The **disadvantages** are:

- Reliance on stability of account managers to provide close personal relationships.
- Neglect of smaller, but high potential accounts.
- Over-reliance on a small number of large accounts.
- Extra information costs (customer profitability, sales by outlet).
- Very high account servicing costs.
- Possible demotivation of sales staff with less glamorous customers.

These four types of sales organisation account for the vast majority of available structures, although many variations are possible. In practice, most high performing companies develop hybrid structures, which combine the best balance between cost and volume of sales.

The important thing is to keep organisation structure constantly under review, looking for creative ways to do things better and create a competitive edge.

Success factors

Organisations do not work automatically. They have to be made to work by following some key principles:

(i) make the organisation functional, to achieve clear objectives;

(ii) make job roles clear at all levels in any change;

(iii) keep it simple from the sales force's point of view;

(iv) keep spans of management control reasonable;

(v) keep the customers' interests in the forefront of any change;

(vi) communicate with and involve all levels in any change, and listen to opinions of sales staff;

(vii) keep support levels strong;

(viii) trade off costs and benefits carefully, particularly when moving towards specialised sales structures;

(ix) constantly reassess workloads at all levels.

Above all, bear in mind the famous quotation of the Roman legionnaire:

'We trained hard, but it seemed that every time we were about to be formed into teams we were reorganised.

'I learnt later in life we tend to meet every situation by reorganising.

'And what a marvellous method it can be for creating the illusion of progress, whilst producing confusion, inefficiency, and demoralisation.'

PETRONIOUS ARBITER, 210 BC

Sales force size

A change of organisation structure and consideration of the new tasks of the sales force at all levels often leads to a review of sales force numbers and deployment.

The simple calculation of sales force size is:

$$\frac{\text{Number of calls per annum} \times \text{call frequency}}{\text{Average call rate/day} \times \text{call days per annum}}$$

If customers are grouped by level of importance, we can produce a grid as follows:

Grouping	Frequency	Time needed	No. of customers
A	2 weekly	3/4 hour	10
B	monthly	1/2 hour	200
C	6 weekly	1/4 hour	500
D	twice a year	1/4 hour	1500

The number of selling hours required is:

$$\underset{(10 \times 25 \times 0.75)}{A} + \underset{(200 \times 120.5)}{B} + \underset{(500 \times 9 \times 0.25)}{C} + \underset{(1500 \times 2 \times 0.25)}{D}$$
$$= \underline{\textbf{3263.5 hours}}$$

If the selling hours per salesperson per annum = *480 hours* (assuming 25 per cent of a working day is face-to-face selling time), then sales force size

$$= \frac{3262.6}{480} = 7$$

You can then calculate the effects of more or fewer sales personnel by break-even analysis. If your average profit margin (contribution) was £10 per unit, and it cost £50,000 to hire or fire a salesperson, you would break even on costs if you sold:

$$\frac{\text{fixed costs}}{\text{contributions}} = \frac{50,000}{10} = 5,000 \text{ units}$$

This means you would need to sell a minimum of 5,000 extra units at £10 contribution per unit to break even on a new salesperson, or lose 5,000 units if you dropped a member of the team. This is a useful method for initial analysis of sales force size. Once sales force sizes are estimated, you can then carry out 'What if' analysis, eg:

- What if we reduced/increased the number of calls?
- What if we changed the call frequency?
- What if we change the time needed per call?
- What if the call rate changed?
- What if we delisted small accounts to wholesalers or distributors?
- What if we increased prospection rates?
- What if we increased servicing by telesales?

Computerised information on sales force activities and costs now enables many companies to analyse sales productivity and make speedy reallocation decisions. However, the majority of companies still rely on occasional manual analysis, or fail to change sales force size and allocation to reflect new conditions.

Organising to exploit potential

This sort of situation often occurs as the dynamics of each sales territory change, as illustrated in Fig. 6.1. The salesperson on Territory 2 may be unable to achieve the target due to adverse trends, while Territory 1 may have plenty of potential but the current salesperson is unable (due to time) or unwilling to exploit it. The solution would be to reorganise accounts or territory boundaries to allow potential in Territory 1 to be exploited. This occurrence is very common, but often the Sales Manager will not address it due to unwillingness to change existing situations, or deal with account reallocations or targeting issues.

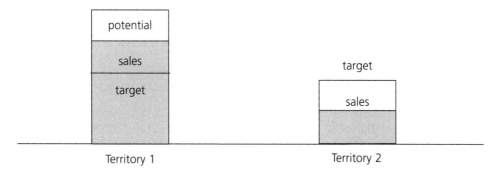

Figure 6.1   Organising to exploit potential

Sales force productivity

Productivity = Relationship between sales output and inputs

Typical desired sales *outputs*:

- volume;
- revenue;
- range;
- mix;
- share;
- gross margin;
- net margin.

Typical sales *inputs* will be:

- type of sales activity (eg field force, telesales, etc.);
- number of sales personnel (outside and inside);
- type of salesperson;

and will be affected by decisions on:

- structuring;
- organisation;
- recruitment;

- training;
- motivation;
- control.

A sales productivity improvement programme has the following stages:

(a) An assessment of the current input/output relationships and their trends.

(b) Reconsideration of desirability/achievability of output targets.

(c) Realignment of input activities to achieve:

- same outputs with less inputs;
- improvement of the input activities to increase productivity.

The key trade-off is between:

Sales (volume/revenue/profit)	**and**	*sales expenses*
relative to target and		relative to budget and
broken down by volume,		affected by numbers,
price and mix		activities and costs

This overall measurement can be further analysed into key productivity measures eg:

(a) sales (revenue/volume) per salesperson;

(b) number of customers/contacts per salesperson;

(c) number of calls per day;

(d) face-to-face time:total time;

(e) orders:calls;

(f) new customer orders:total orders;

(g) average order value (new/old customers);

(h) 'direct', sales costs:total sales costs;

(i) % labour turnover;

(j) sales per trained person:sales per untrained person;

(k) most successful salesperson:average salesperson.

A systematic programme for improving sales productivity[1]

1 Decide the key measurements in the business in terms of the cause-effect relationships involved.

2 Analyse the current situation against the past, across the sales force and versus comparable situations.

3 Reassess the desired and achievable outputs required in terms of what results, from whom.

4 Establish what has to be done to persuade them to buy.

5 Categorise customers in terms of their service requirements.

6 Consider how those services can be most cost-effectively provided - either internally and/or externally.

7 Structure the sales activity to reflect the nature, scale and requirements of the customer groups to be served.

8 Organise the sales activity on the basis of workload and to maximise selling time.

9 Improve the recruitment process to provide the maximum number of sales personnel with the potential to be highly effective.

10 Construct training programmes which accurately reflect the sales task to be performed.

11 Check the motivational environment – using research where necessary – and create appropriate financial and non-financial incentives.

12 Monitor productivity performance against pre-set criteria regularly.

13 Search for productivity improvement from a better understanding of the buyer/seller relationships.

14 Use technology to free sales force time for redeployment on more creative activities.

[1] Source: M. T. Wilson, *Managing a Sales Force*, Gower Press, 1983.

CHECKPOINTS

■ How market-focused is your sales organisation?

■ How cost effective is your sales structure?

■ How can you improve organisational effectiveness and productivity?

CHAPTER SEVEN

Recruitment and selection

Although recruitment of sales staff is only a periodic task for Sales Managers, mistakes at any stage can be very expensive.

- Recruiting the wrong person results in lost business and customers and expensive recruitment costs.
- Failing to recruit the right candidate allows quality staff to go to competitors.
- If appointees leave quickly, heavy costs of recruitment recur.

This chapter concentrates on ways to reduce the error rate. Mistakes will still occur, but they can be minimised by careful methods.

Selection process

The recruitment process follows the following steps:

(1) Accurate job description.

(2) Person profile.

(3) Attracting candidates.

(4) Screening replies.

(5) Interviewing/testing.

(6) Appointment.

(7) Reference checking.

1. Job description

This must be up-to-date and accurate for the job vacancy, following good practice such as:

- short in length
- simple language
- tasks clearly explained in priority order
- relates tasks to performance standards, not general loose statements, eg instead of 'maintains regular contact with territory customers', it is better to say: 'visits four to six small business customers per day and one major customer, with at least 50 per cent orders to calls made'.

2. Person profile[1]

This is the key recruitment stage, as the profile influences the whole of the remaining process. Much care should be taken to write down all the required criteria, and to be clear whether each is 'desirable' or 'essential'. A typical list of profile criteria would be:

Profile criteria

(Code factors 'desirable' or 'essential')

'Can do' factors

1 *Appearance and impact*

2 *Measurable factors*

- – Age

- – Experience

- – Education (including professional qualifications)

- – Special qualifications

---

[1] Checklists in this Chapter are reproduced by kind permission of M. T. Wilson, *Managing a Sales Force*, Gower Press, 1983.

- Intelligence

- Availability

- Driving licence

- Health

- Location

'Will do' factors

3 *Character traits – need for*

- Stability (maintaining same job and interests)

- Industry (willingness to work)

- Perseverance (finishing what he or she starts)

- Ability to get along with others

- Loyalty

- Self-reliance

- Leadership

4 *Job motivations (not already satisfied off the job) need for*

- Money

- Security

- Status

- Power

- Perfection

- To compete

- To serve

- For job satisfaction:

  (i)   work itself

  (ii) recognition

    (iii) to achieve

    (iv) for advancement

    (v) for personal responsibility and growth

5 *Degree of emotional maturity*

- Independence

- Regard of consequences

- Capacity for self-discipline

- Individualism

- Extraversion

- Outside interests

- Willingness to accept responsibility

Many of these factors can be measured accurately by procedures, using specialist psychologists and known tests. The best performing sales staff can be 'profiled' to identify what they have in common, so that criteria can be placed in priority order for the recruitment process. These tests are widespread and can cover personality, behaviour, mental ability or job skills. They also remove much of the subjectivity of interview techniques, where big mistakes can be made in assessing candidates' qualities.

'A deeper behavioural profile of past experience is one of the best predictors of future performance. You can teach a turkey to climb trees, but it's better to hire a squirrel.'

PATRICIA MARSHALL, HAY/McBER

What makes a good salesperson?

Each company must do its own analysis of high performers to find out what characteristics work for them, but American researchers, Mayer and Greenberg, found that successful selling depended on just two qualities:

- **empathy**, ie the ability to feel as others feel;

- **ego drive**, a strong inner motivation to succeed.

They found that sales staff were less successful if:

(i)   high on empathy, low on ego drive – poor closers of sales;

(ii) high on ego drive, low on empathy – poor listeners, upset customers;

(iii) low on empathy and ego drive – invariably unsuccessful.

Various tests exist that profile sales candidates and can be tailored to individual companies. Two examples of these are PASAT (Poppleton Allan Sales Aptitude Test) and SST International, which focuses on sales skills which can be improved.

Profile pitfalls

- Do not be obsessed with age limits – youth may be desirable, but could older candidates still do the job?

- Be realistic on industry experience or product knowledge. Selling skills are often more valuable than industry experience or product knowledge, which can be taught. You may need fresh eyes to your business.

- Are qualifications vital? To sell houses, do you need to be a surveyor? To sell engineering products, do you need to be a qualified engineer?

- Reduce the number of 'essential' criteria – perfect candidates rarely exist, and too narrow a profile will reduce response rates significantly.

- Do not neglect basic criteria at the first stage, eg health, clean driving licence, location.

- Beware of the profile being a mirror image of yourself – candidates with different qualities may well be able to succeed.

3. Attracting candidates

Candidates may come from:

- Company's own staff
- Referrals from existing staff or customers
- Agencies
- Advertising.

1 **Headline and advert design** to create interest

2 **Precise location** (re-location assistance improves response rates)

3 **Salary and rewards** mentioned specifically will increase response rates and target the advert to expectations of reward

4 Five structured elements of the advert

  A **Company information**

  B **Job information**

  C **Candidate profile information** – presented with novelty in this example

  D **Reward benefits** information

  E **Action information** – named person and telephone number increases response rates and speeds up the process

5 **Company name** increases response rates, so try to avoid box numbers, or general Company descriptions

Agencies: There are many specialist recruitment agencies for sales personnel, who charge either a fixed fee or a percentage of salary for successful recruitment.

Advertising: This is by far the most common method of attracting a pool of candidates. Figure 7.1 shows all the points necessary to produce high response rates for suitably qualified candidates. Even with high unemployment rates, good candidates usually have more than one choice, so it is important to sell the Company at the first stage.

Media should be chosen after consulting an advertising agency or media owner, who will provide circulation and response rates for analysis.

The following advert has all the elements necessary to achieve a successful response. Failure to include all these points in any advert will reduce response rates, often significantly.

4. Screening replies

It is important to act with speed in the recruitment process, both to impress candidates and to fill jobs quickly. Responses should be collected via application forms or a curriculum vitae, but an immediate *telephone screen* is the best first step – hence the recommendation to put telephone numbers in adverts.

Good candidates can be invited for interview quickly by this method, and short-lists set up within days. Sending in CVs or application forms can take weeks, and sometimes good candidates receive other offers in that time.

The following is an example of a telephone screen form (Fig. 7.2). This can be completed by administrative staff, but is best done by the Sales Manager, so making time for this activity is important.

Figure 7.1 (pg 92) Effective recruitment advertisement.

Reproduced by kind permission of Colgate-Palmolive, Michael Page Marketing and Nucleus Advertising Ltd. Copy and design by Nucleus.

TELEPHONE SCREENING FORM

DATE ——————— JOB APPLIED FOR ————————————

1 May I have your name? ————————————————

2 Your address where you can be contacted? —————————

3 Telephone numbers where you can be contacted? When?
Day-time ——————————————————————
Night-time —————————————————————

4 Why are you looking for a new job? ——————————

5 What are you doing now? ———————————————
Who for? ———————————————————————
(Is it good experience for this job?)
How long ———————————————— *(Good company? Stable?)*

6 And before that? —————————————————
Who for? ———————————————————————
(Is it good experience/ Progression? Good company?)
How long? ——————————————————————

7 What are you earning now? —————————————
(Must be realistic)

8 What do you expect to earn? ————————————
(Must be in line with that offered)

9 What ties do you have with regard to location? —————

10 When can you be available? ——————————————

(Is that soon enough?)

11 Age? ——————————————————————

12 What qualifications do you have? ——————————

Completed by ——————————————————————
Immediate interview?   Yes/No

Figure 7.2   Telephone screening form

5. Interviewing/testing

Sales Managers often regard themselves as having interview skills as 'natural gifts', or simply because they are managers. In fact, research has shown that the majority of people are poor interviewers, and that decisions such as personnel selection based on unskilled interviews are extremely risky. Interviewing is a major part of inter-personal competence, and deeply affects:

- The 'image' a manager has.
- The quality and quantity of information given and received.
- The effectiveness of decisions.
- Use of time.
- Persuasiveness.

The process

As the objective is to exchange information, the process can be divided into two parts:

(i)   the conduct of the interview

(ii) the assessment of the information.

Obviously, the ability to do (i) will greatly affect the success of (ii). By looking at the factors which determine the success of an interview, we may be able to see whether good interviewers are 'born' or 'made'.

A good interview tends to be one conducted with

- preparation and objectives (*purpose*)
- alertness and concentration (*listen*)
- persistence, but politeness (*control*)
- warmth and empathy (*rapport*)
- freedom from bias (*objectivity*)

Whereas some people will naturally make better interviewers than others, it is also obvious that these skills can be improved by training.

Preparation

Always collect as much information as possible about the interviewee and the objectives of the interview, and analyse this beforehand. Set out clearly the areas where you need more detail and use this in preparing the strategy of the interview.

An opening should be carefully prepared as the initial few minutes will often set the style for the whole interview. An interviewee needs to feel relaxed so that a two-way exchange can be assured. It is sometimes useful to start with questions which you know the interviewee can answer (after the opening pleasantries) so that he or she begins to talk immediately and feels more confident.

A series of topic areas and questions should be prepared so that the interviewer can guide the interview, ask the same questions of each candidate, and write down replies.

Establishing rapport

An interviewer who is concerned with eliciting truth openly will not make headway unless interviews are based on the recognition that *only secure people can risk change*. Hence the need to establish rapport, confidence and security in the interview before proceeding to explore considerations which might be threatening. Most interviewees (and interviewers!) are initially defensive in interview situations, protecting their self-image, so how can rapport be established?

- Adopt warm, friendly manner, eye-contact and smile. (Nervous, unprepared interviewers do *not* make people feel secure.)
- Treat the other as an equal – eliminate social biases; do not 'dominate' or be pompous. (See 'communication barriers' below.)
- Establish a smooth and easy pattern of interaction.
- Find some common interest, experience, etc.
- Give full attention, show there is plenty of time, that you know details and have an interest in the person.

Some basic techniques to raise conversation and get candidates talking are:

- Open-ended questions, eg what, how, why, where, when etc. (not questions which elicit yes or no responses).
- Agreement, encouragement and follow-up of points – use of summaries of points (remember – non-verbal communication).

- Use of silence (actively use it).
- Pay attention to 'feeling' statements.

Avoiding communication barriers

An equilibrium must be established in the interview so that the styles of behaviour of both interviewer and interviewee synchronise. Much of the responsibility for this lies with the interviewer. He or she must learn:

- *to be neutral* – concealing biases, attitudes and prejudices. In particular, beware of first impressions or 'halo effects' – if you like a candidate you will tend to like everything, and if you dislike a candidate, you will tend to dislike everything. Both these effects can give wrong readings of candidates, thus increasing error rates.
- *to avoid signals of boredom*, impatience and intolerance which the interviewee might pick up.
- *to understand non-verbal communications* and to use them positively to help the process. These signals include:
  - body language;
  - proximity (eg remove desk barriers);
  - orientation;
  - appearance;
  - head-nods;
  - facial expression;
  - posture;
  - eye movements;
  - non-verbal aspects of speech-timing, emotional tone;
  - speech errors.

These non-verbal elements are used to manage interpersonal relationships in a partly-conscious, more-or-less spontaneous way. They express *emotions*, attitudes towards the other, and *self-image*; they are used to control the timing of speech and to help maintain the relationship.

- Always *start the interview (following pleasantries) with an outline of the job*, interview format, and what you both want to achieve. Make occasional summaries as the interview progresses so that you can be sure you understood the interviewee and be corrected if you made the wrong interpretation.

- Always *listen to what is being said*, do not anticipate what *will be* said and become impatient for the interviewee to stop talking so that you can ask further questions.

- *Pursue points in depth* by asking supplementary probing questions and check answers against any previous information you have obtained.

- Always *ask the interviewee for questions to ask you* so the interview is not one-sided.

- Always *finish the interview with a short summary*, further job information, and discuss what the next course of action will be.

Some typical errors

The following are some typical errors made in interviewing, and their consequences. As can be appreciated, poor running of an interview will result in poor information exchange. The consequent assessment of person or situation is thus seriously affected.

Error	Consequences
No preparation	No strategy – unclear objective. Difficult to establish smooth pattern. Unable to show early interviewee interest.
Asking leading questions	Prevents interviewee 'opening up'; prevents 'cues' to further questions; eliminates 'depth'; prevents rapport.
Giving opinions and judgements	Inhibits openness and further objectivity; may make interviewee guarded – irrelevant.
Not pursuing points in depth	Prevents insight into interviewee, and checking-out of stated 'facts'.
Asking challenging questions too early	Prevents rapport; may create anxiety and nervousness with loss of security.
Interviewer talks too much	Interviewer will feel 'good' – interviewee will agree with him . . . interviewee good! Total art of interview is listening and direction with careful open-ended questions. Talking is *not* control.

Bias incorporated	Prevents objectivity and clear assessment *vis-à-vis* job. If interviewee detects it, loss of rapport or facile agreement.
Not getting at the facts	Poor understanding of interviewee. Interviewer may be 'fooled'. Superficial exchange.
Wasting time	Diversion.
Lack of summaries of points	Fails to give the interviewee sense of structure and understanding by interviewer. Leads to wrong conclusion.

Structuring the interview

Questions should be asked only to help identify profile criteria, as in the following chart (Fig. 7.3):

Specific questions can be asked of every candidate (to ensure consistency), and modified by experience, or guided by established test questions produced by psychologists. Examples would be:

1 How did you get into Sales?

2 What do you most enjoy and hate doing in the job?

3 What are your ambitions?

4 Why this job?

5 What are your strengths and weaknesses?

6 What motivates you?

7 What annoys you?

8 What is your greatest achievement?

9 What people do you like or dislike?

10 How do you plan your time?

11 What do you know about us?

12 What gives you most difficulty in achieving sales?

MOTIVATIONS

Source of evidence	Material	Security	Status
Family background	Strong or weak finances at home? Attitude of parents to money. Any of own money earned?	Stable family background? Parentally? Location?	Socially conscious family?
Edudational history	Interested in financial subjects? Earned own money whilst studying? Got qualifications in order to get more money?	Kept to same subjects because felt secure? Chose only things he or she knew and and could do well?	Schools and colleges selected for status rather than educational achievement? Chose status courses?
Work experience	Sought high-paying jobs? Paid by results? Left jobs because of money?	Sought safe salaried jobs? Chose large companies? Enjoyed structure?	Picked status job with prestige companies? Enjoys status titles? Exaggerates level of job?
Outside interests	Increases earnings with part-time work? Makes money out of leisure interests?	Enjoys home-based leisure interests? Avoids dangerous sports, etc?	Chooses prestigious interests? Enjoys being council member, church warden, etc?
Domestic situation	Good standard of living within income? Expensive tastes?	Stable home environment? Low ambition?	Needs social status? Climbers? Children must go to right schools?
Expressed desires	Wants this job simply for pay? Wiling to sacrifice to make more money? Ambition to be rich?	Wants this job because of career possibilities? Does not want to move or travel?	Wants job because of prestige? Wants to achieve social position in business?

Figure 7.3   Interviewing – possible (but *not* obligatory) questions

(N.B. Beware of the effect of your own beliefs/values in evaluating answers)

MOTIVATIONS *(continued)*

Power	Perfection	Competitiveness	Service
Was father or mother powerful? Did they exercise power at home?	Encouraged to perfection in manners, dress, behaviour?	Large or small family? Complete with brothers and sisters?	Encouraged to serve others? Church/ Scout type activities?
Enjoyed being most senior because of power? Wanted to learn because of power?	Enjoyed research and detail subjects?	Enjoyed competing to be top of class or best at sport? Chose competitive situations – scholarships, awards, prizes, etc.?	Worked for school? Helped others whilst at school?
Likes to dominate colleagues, juniors, customers? Wants bigger job even though money similar?	Likes detail work? Wants job done well?	Enjoys competition from colleagues and other companies? Compares with others?	Chose socially rewarding work? Wants jobs that contribute to community? Enjoys helping customers?
Enjoys power in outside interests? Sought chairman positions, captain, president, etc?	Indicates desire for perfection, eg model-building? Rose-growing, etc?	Chooses interests eg individual sports, enters competitions and shows?	Charity work? Social or church work? Helping others, eg Scout-master, part-time teacher?
Enjoys being boss in own home? Attempts to decide children's future? children?	Spends much time improving house and garden? Over-diciplined at everything?	Enjoys discussion with family and friends? Wants children to be best	Works for family rather than self? Encourages family in social work?
Sees job as giving power? Enjoys power of decision over whether to take job?	Wants to do good job in detail? Asks lots of questions about job? Detailed application form? success in competitive terms?	Wants to know who will compete with in future? Interested in sales contests? Regards satisfaction?	Wants to know about customers and what they want? Sees success in terms of customer

DEGREE OF EMOTIONAL MATURITY

Source of evidence	Independence	Regard for consequences	Capacity for self-discipline
Family background	Overdominant parents? Not allowed to make own decisions? Only child?	Parental concern for education? Poor choice of school, etc?	Never had to concentrate on studies or leisure activities?
Educational history	Always guided by someone? and later regretted it?	Left school too early? Dropped subjects	Could not study? Took easy options?
Work experience	Advised into career? Sought structured jobs? Changed job because of pressure from friends or family? Happy to be career salesperson?	Chose wrong career to start? Left jobs without having employment? Promised customers impossibilities? Talks at interviews without thinking of implications?	Despite warnings unable to meet previous job standards of punctuality, report-writing, etc?
Outside interests	Chooses highly structured situations?	Has allowed outside interests to interfere with main job?	Has allowed interests to lapse because can't be bothered to fit them in?
Domestic situation	Highly reliant on family? Likes quiet structured home life?	Spend more than can afford? Has too big a family, too big commitments? Lives beyond income?	Allows family to decide what should be done?
Expressed desires	Wants job because big secure company? Does not want to move or travel? Interested in own supervision and training?	Does not know why wants job? Has not thought through career? Resigned before got job?	Does not handle self well at interviews? Badly prepared? Shows feeling easily?

Figure 7.3   Continued

DEGREE OF EMOTIONAL MATURITY *(continued)*

Individualism	Extraversion	Outside interests	Willingness to accept responsibility
Did what wanted to? Left home when wanted to?	Enjoyed showing off? Encouraged to do so by parents?	Never developed interests?	Never had to face responsibility?
Thought only of self? No regard paid to parent's interests?	Enjoyed activities such as dramatics, debating?	Avoided studies or interests that took up leisure time?	Sees failure at school as someone else's fault? Never held positions of responsibility?
Took job decisions without considering or consulting family? Sees previous employers only from own point of view? Only interested in how new job affects self personally?	Enjoys public demonstrations, display work? Shows off in dress, manner? Talks of own achievements? Talks too much and too loud?	Dislikes hard work? Dislikes interference with leisure time? Enjoys trips, drink, food, golf too much?	Previous job failure always someone else's fault? Avoids positions of responsibility?
Follows personal interests contrary to family interests?	Chosen interest where can show off?	Interests limited to self-indulgence, drinking, gambling, eating?	No interests with any responsibility?
Has considered amily when choosing jobs? Time away from home? Relocation?	Is the 'life and soul' of the party? Enjoys showing off with friends?	Are home activities all leisure-orientated? Spends a lot of time at the pub, parties, etc?	Allow others to dominate? Who decides family holidays, children's schooling, etc?
All questions asked relate to self? Not interested in company and its future, or colleagues?	Shows off at interview in dress, manner, speech? Claims vast achievements? major achieve-ments in that area?	Asks mainly about holiday and working hours? Enjoys talking about leisure pursuits? Sees family and friends on all points?	Wants help and advice on career? Finds it difficult to decide on job? Wants to consult

PERSONALITY

Source of evidence	Stability	Industry	Perseverance
Family background	Stable childhood? Parents together? Stable location?	Encouraged to work at home? Keep busy during leisure time?	Encouraged to continue with studies, etc? Has hobbies that needed time and care?
Educational history	Same school? Same courses? Signs of growth and development of ideas?	Work hard at school? Success? Choose demanding leisure interests? Any self-motivated ? study	Follow through courses started? Further education? Continued interests?
Work experience	Changed jobs? Changed type of work? Changed location? Good reasons for leaving?	Chosen hard or soft jobs? Attitude to hours of work, travelling?	Has work demanded perseverance? Continued trying in difficult circumstances?
Outside interests	Continued same interests? Played sports with same people?	Do interests need work, eg council, committees. Need effort, eg vigorous sports?	Worked way up in social activity, eg committee head?
Domestic situation	Marital status? Family? Time away from home? situation?	Work at home? Developed personal financial	Built up strong family and financial position?
Expressed desires	Wants to stay in same location? Same type of work? Dislikes travelling? Sees career opportunity?	Sees challenge of job? Prepared for long hours and arduous work? Willing to take further training?	Determined to succeed? Building up long-term prospects?

Figure 7.3   Continued

PERSONALITY *(continued)*

Ability to get along with others	Loyalty	Self-reliance	Leadership
Big or small family? Group or solitary pursuits?	Indentifies with parents and background?	Encouraged to stand on own feet? When left home?	Any positions of leadership eg Scouts? Youth Club Leader?
Take part in group activities? Enjoy group activities?	Attitude to school and/or college? Particular teachers?	Succeed on own? Earn own expenses?	Positions of responsibility – in school? – sports? – social? – college or university?
Attitude to customers? To colleagues? To others?	Loyal to previous employers? Team worker? Willingness to accept management?	Found own jobs? Chosen jobs where on own? Enjoyed making own decisions?	Any positions of leaderships? Ambitions?
Groups or solitary positions activities, eg team games, societies or fishing, stamp collecting?	Stayed with same groups and teams? Attitudes to societies and associations?	Interests require self-reliance, eg climbing, sailing, acting?	Leadership in outside interests
Marital relations? Attitude to relatives and friends?	Loyalty to relatives and friends?	Makes decisions at home? Self-financing? Working partner?	Dominant partner?
Sees teamwork needed? Dept preferred because of other people? Dislikes loneliness of travel? Get along with you?	Wants job because all previous companies misunderstood?	Wants job for own reasons? Will go anywhere any time? Confident of ability to do job?	Looking for management job? Prepared to train formanagement?

How many interviews?

Most sales force selection decisions are taken after a two-stage approach:

First interview of up to ten candidates for each position. This would normally be a one-to-one interview (to create a more relaxed atmosphere), aimed at screening candidates to a final short list of three or four per position. Always keep a reserve list of applicants on hold in case the first selections prove unsuitable.

Second interview which should be much more intensive and could involve:

- Sales Manager, Sales Director and Personnel Manager.

- Meeting members of the sales team.

- Presenting on a project completed between the two interviews, eg 'How would you develop a sales plan for a new product?' or 'How would you develop the distributor market on your territory?'

- An Assessment Centre, using profile tests and interpretation by a psychologist and a range of practical individual/team exercises. These are particularly important if trying to recruit sales staff for long-term career development.

6. Appointment

The most effective way to rate all candidates fairly is to draw up a Company placement form, comprising all the profile criteria and a rating scale (Fig. 7.4). This removes most subjectivity from the decision and ensures fairness to all candidates.

Intuition can be considered, but not relied on fully. Big mistakes have been made based on poor intuition or 'gut feel'.

PLACEMENT

Applicant's name

Factors (examples)	RATING	WEIGHT*	WEIGHTED SCORE	COMMENTS
A Quantative factors 1 2 3 4				
1 Age				
2 Education				
3 Exerience				
4 Special qualifications				
5 Intelligence				
6 Availability				
7 Health				
8 Location				
B Character traits				
1 Stability				
2 Industry				
3 Perseverance				
4 Ability to get along with others				
5 Loyalty				
6 Self-reliance				
7 Leadership				
C Motivations				
1 Money				
2 Security				
3 Status				
4 Power				
5 Perfection				
6 Competitiveness				
7 Service				
D Degree of emotional maturity				
1 Independence				
2 Regard of consequences				
3 Capacity for self-discipline				
4 Individualism				
5 Extraversion				
6 Outside interests				
7 Willingness to accept responsibility				
OVERALL COMMENT				
RECOMMENDATION			Rated by	

Rating Scale: 4. Meets requirements fully   3. Better than average   2. Marginal   1. Poor

* Divide 100 points to the selected factors in the left column, eg Age 5, Achievement 15, Status 2, etc. Multiply the score (1–4) by each weight to get a weighted score. The total will be out of 400 (100 × 4) maximum.

Figure 7.4   Example of placement form

7. References

This is the vital last stage of recruitment, and should not be neglected. Candidates could have falsified information given on the application form/CV, and a view from previous bosses is always useful.

Two horror stories illustrate the problem.

(i) In reference checking, one salesperson's current Manager said he did the job well, but could never be contacted on Friday afternoons!

On probing, the salesman revealed he worked in his wife's hairdressing business and would not give it up. His job offer was withdrawn.

(ii) Another Sales Manager had a telephone call from a competitor's Sales Manager: 'Could we have Mr X's leaving documents as he has been with us two months and we have not received them?' The first Sales Manager was surprised, as the salesman was still working for him! It turned out that the salesman worked unsupervised in a remote territory and was drawing two salaries and two company cars. No one had asked for references.

References should be requested when the job offer is made, 'subject to references'. Two previous bosses are best. The candidate is informed he or she must resign from the current employer, so the references can be taken up at the candidate's risk. Keep other possible candidates on hold, in case the appointment falls through.

Telephone checks are best, but some companies will not give them other than in writing. The emphasis should be on factual accuracy, not opinions, as candidates may be able to sue successfully for damaging opinions from a previous employer.
Specific questions would include:

- Dates of employment.
- Types of selling involved.
- Customers handled.
- Salary/commission earned.
- Absenteeism.
- Sales success (eg 'Was he Salesman of the Month three times last year?').

Conclusion

The methods listed in this chapter will help to reduce the error rate in a very expensive process, and help to select the right candidates, while not selecting the wrong ones.

Research shows conclusively that top performing companies using systematic well-defined recruitment methods consistently out-perform those who rely too heavily on haphazard 'gut feel' methods.

Finally, remember that recruitment is two way. Many candidates offered jobs, after an exhaustive process, turn them down. The reason is that companies have failed in the very area for which they are recruiting – they have failed to sell themselves to the best candidates.

CHECKPOINTS

- How can you improve the quality of your salesforce recruitment process?
- How can you improve and test the quality of your salesperson profile?
- How can you improve the quality of your interviewing process and skills?

CHAPTER EIGHT

Coaching and training

Coaching and training should be the prime responsibility and task of first-line Sales Managers, as results are achieved through the attitude, skill and knowledge (ASK) development of the team.

In practice, rarely is sufficient time and effort made available by Sales Managers to coach and train effectively. Indeed, some Sales Managers have poor attitudes towards the whole subject.

> *'They should train themselves.'*
>
> *'They can spend a few days with an experienced salesperson, then we leave them alone.'*
>
> *'If they are no good we fire them.'*
>
> *'I don't like interfering.'*
>
> *'Customers do not like Sales Managers to accompany sales staff.'*
>
> *'Sales people like to be left alone.'*
>
> *'I feel exposed if I try to train them.'*
>
> *'Sales people are born, not made.'*
>
> *'We only recruit fully trained people.'*
>
> *'There's no substitute for experience.'*

In fact, research shows that these statements are fallacious, and that training well done is an investment of time well worth making.

'For Sales Managers, developing others' abilities is even more important – indeed it's the emotional competence most frequently found among those at the top of the field. This is a person-to-person art, and the effectiveness of counselling hinges on empathy and the ability to focus on our own feelings and show them.'
'WORKING WITH EMOTIONAL INTELLIGENCE', DANIEL GOLEMAN, BLOOMSBURY

Benefits

The benefits of training are:

- Improved sales results.
- Overcoming competition.
- Satisfied customers.
- Improved motivation.
- Reduced staff turnover.
- Reduced recruitment time.
- Improved new trainee productivity.
- Grown management.

All training and coaching follows the training cycle, as follows (Fig. 8.1)

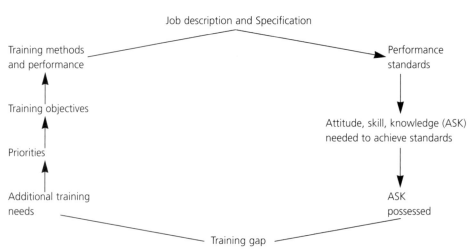

Figure 8.1   Identifying training needs

Learning principles

Learning means improving standards of knowledge, skill and attitude and being able to apply them in the work situation.

Learning works as follows:

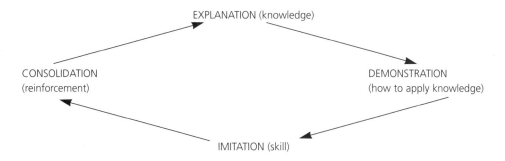

This is a continuous process, and many companies fail to train sales staff properly because they adopt superficial policies on training. Successful Sales Managers apply the **3 R's** of training:

1 **Repetition.** Attitudes, Skills and Knowledge (ASK) must be repeated to be remembered. This works on the mind like advertising – repeated messages are learnt, and once learnt are actioned successfully.

It is clear that a single training programme or coaching event will produce little learning but repeated events will succeed. Good coaches constantly repeat training in knowledge (eg quizzes), skills (eg practice role plays) and attitude (eg projects), creating variety and enjoyment in learning. Repetition applies to sales management training, as well as sales training, of course, so coaching needs to be practised repetitively.

Generic coaching processes which rely on ownership and empowerment for success often fall short because the learning is not tested. It is easy to say, for example, 'I will improve my customer questioning skills', but only practice of skills or knowledge testing will create the embedded learning. Sales staff may 'talk a good game', but only practice makes perfect. The famous soccer player, Eric Cantona, said that repeated practice enabled him to draw on the skill when needed, so that it became 'unconscious competence'.

2 **Reinforcement**. This is the prime role of field, or on-the-job, training usually termed coaching. Observation and job-related practise of ASK encourages learning by doing and reinforces the message in real life situations after learning from off-the-job (course) training.

3 **Recognition**. Successful ASK progress should be recognised and rewarded motivationally, by recording progress and relating development to personal growth and a career plan. Peer group recognition of ASK development is an excellent motivator, and works on a 'cascade' basis at every job level. (see 'Coaching Control').

People learn best and change behaviour when there is:

(a) *Connection* – of new input with existing ASK.

(b) *Logical progression* from one level to the next (building blocks).

(c) *Variety* in methods, participation, creativity and chance to practise.

(d) *'Bite-sized pieces'* – a bit of learning at a time.

Induction training

New recruits to a sales team, even if experienced, require proper induction into the Company. The Sales Manager should follow core training principles in creating a tailored programme for each recruit.

- What do they need to know, understand or be able to do?
- What should the pace of training be?
- How can progress be monitored?

Often induction programmes are poorly planned and implemented, and sometimes do not exist at all!

A typical induction programme would be:

Week 1	Head Office departments
	Administration
	Product knowledge and sales skills training (off-job)
	Selling standards/job elements
	Demonstration in field (one day)
Week 2	Role plays (skill development)
	Study assignments
	Demonstration calls
	Works alone (one day)
Week 3	Trainee works alone
Week 4	Dual calling with Sales Manager (coaching) (three days)
	Sole calling (two days)
Week 5	Sole calling
Week 6	Dual calling
	Study assignment
	Demonstration
Week 7	Sole calling
Week 8	Dual calling
	Knowledge testing
	Training report
	Future training/review

Programmes can be laid down for up to two years ahead, and cover refresher training, advanced selling, qualifications, projects, etc.

In some industries (notably financial services) trainees can reach different levels of ASK, and be 'certificated' as achieving defined standards.

Coaching/field training

Coaching is the usual term used to describe *on-the-job training*. *Off-the-job training* will be discussed in the chapter on Sales Meetings.

Coaching aims

(a) Assess performance against agreed job definition and standards.

(b) Determine and agree development areas.

(c) Coach in skills and techniques agreed.

(d) Build positive attitudes in selling by example, encouragement and instruction.

(e) Give specific guidance in ongoing self-training.

(f) Determine training needs which cannot be done in the field, and how to tackle them.

(g) Estimate performance improvements and effect of training.

The Sales Manager coaches by having a defined set of ASK standards in each part of the job, often written down in a *Sales Manual*. This is good sales management practice, as it promotes job clarity – a great motivator, as discussed earlier.

Benefits of sales manual

- Develops job description into necessary attitude, skills and knowledge.
- Provides source material of *how* the job should be done.
- Helps at all levels of training:
    - induction (off-the-job);
    - refresher (on-the-job).
- Provides basis of performance appraisal system, linked to standards of achievement in each job area.

Sales manual content (Example)

1 Company background

2 Our markets/customers

3 The selling role

4 Selling skills

- opening

- presentation

- objections

- close

- merchandising

- promotions

5 Territory management

- journey planning

- territory and customer management

- call planning/preparation

Product knowledge is usually included in a separate product manual, giving features and benefits of each product in the range and competitive product information.

Sales manuals are excellent projects for involving the sales force. Each person can write a chapter, with the Sales Manager co-ordinating style and content. Ownership is achieved, thus increasing commitment to achieve defined standards.

Job aspects/structure

Coaching works best when the whole job is clearly broken down into smaller parts, as learning works best on a 'building block' approach.

An example would be:

1 Functional	**2** Sales skills
(a) Use of time	approach
starting	decision-maker
pre-call preparation	opening
journey planning	control
rest breaks	listening
waiting times	needs/problems
relationships	creativity
stock checks	objections

(b) Tasks

preparation

call sequence

call rate

conversion rate

order size

administration/others

benefits

communications

closing

sales aids

knowledge

3 **Organisation**

information/records

sales aids check

appointments

car

tidiness/accessibility

briefcase

administration

communications

commitments/follow-up

4 **Attitude**

warmth

empathy

enthusiasm

loyalty

positiveness

team spirit

As recommended in Chapter 1, each salesperson should receive at least one full day of coaching per month (on-the-job). This can be increased significantly for new appointees, and reduced for more experienced staff, although even very good sales staff should be coached – it motivates; allows feedback; gives the Sales Manager new ideas; leads to developmental training; and stops attrition of skills due to complacency. More time on coaching will never be wasted.

Requirements of a good Sales Coach

- Good selling skills for credibility (but not necessarily the best in the team).
- Full understanding of the sales structure and ASK standards.
- Analytical ability.
- Empathy and understanding.
- Creativity in methods used.
- Skill in all training techniques.
- Enthusiasm and motivation.

A good analogy is sports coaches, who should have all the analysis and motivational skills, but who are rarely better than their protégés at 'doing' it correctly in practice. The skill is in selecting the right methods to achieve behavioural change, which will improve sales results. Sales Managers as coaches can reduce the spread between the best and worst sales performers in the team, by embedding best practices in a relentless 3 R's process. This can be visualized as follows:

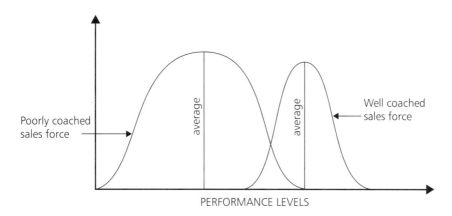

The coaching process - six steps

Before the call

STEP 1 *Analysis*
- when was the last call?
- which products were covered?
- what objections were raised?
- which products were sold?
- which were not sold?
- what information was gained?

STEP 2 *Plan and prepare the call*
- what are the call *objectives*?
- what are the customer's *needs*?
- what *products* are to be covered and in what order?
- how will the call be *opened*?

- what *sales aids* will be used?
- which *benefits* will be mentioned and in what order?
- what *facts* will be used to support the benefits?
- what *questions* will be asked to check customer agreement?
- what are the likely *objections* and how will they be handled?
- how will the call be *closed*?
- *rehearse* any aspects of the call (role-play)

STEP 3   *Agree what part you will both take in the call*
- demonstration call
- observation of whole by you
- joint selling role
- help if requested or necessary to achieve sales result

During the call

STEP 4   *Watch and listen*
- avoid being drawn in by the customer
- look at the salesperson not at the customer (sit to one side)
- avoid unplanned intervention
- look for diversions from the agreed plan
- what reasons were there for them?
- what effect did they have on the outcome?
- is the commercial situation as envisaged?
- is the objective achieved?
- what weaknesses are there in the presentation?
- what improvements since the last call?
- what is being done well?

After the call

STEP 5   *Analyse the performance*

Follow a sequence:
- first praise in detail all the things done well
- question to get critical self-analysis (see checklist, Fig. 8.2)
- help identify any training needs

QUESTIONING METHODS

Five levels of information	Examples (not sequential)
Level 1 SITUATION INFORMATION focused into	'How do you think that went?' 'What was the customer's real worry?'
Level 2 ISSUES/PROBLEMS INFORMATION summarised and amplified into	'Why was that?' 'How do you think he feels now?' 'Why did he say that?'
Level 3 EFFECT/IMPLICATIONS INFORMATION	'What should we have asked the customer?' How would that have helped?' 'How would that help us in other interviews?'
Level 4 TRAINING NEEDS INFORMATION expanded into and agreed	'So it would help if we were able to …?' 'You would feel more confident if …?'
Level 5 TRAINING SOLUTIONS INFORMATION agreed verbally and recorded in the Sales Training Plan	'The way we could do it is …?' 'You agree it would help if …?'

Figure 8.2   Coaching process – 5 steps analysis of performance checklist

- gain acceptance of needs
- show how to improve by practice/demonstration
- agree follow-up/self-learning
- encourage

STEP 6

- set specific recorded training objectives for the next visit, at the end of this visit, and agree time plan for review
- complete coaching checklist of ASK with sales person.

Coaching – Ten practical ideas towards successful sales management

1 Coaching is an *excuse to develop selling skills* using a 'random' sales interview as a live vehicle.

2 It is a prime *motivational* opportunity, so try to build and praise, not criticise.

3 Coaching *reinforces* off-the-job training, so use a *selling model* which is consistent and can be learnt by repetition/ practice.

Customer Buying Process	Selling Stages	Selling Steps
1 I am important	1 Rapport building	These steps will follow the sequential methods within each Stage (see example, page 44–46)
2 Consider my needs	2. Questioning	
3 How can you help?	3. Presentation	
4 What are the facts?		
5 What are the snags?	4. Objection handling	
6 What should I do?		
7 I agree	5. Commitment	
8 I'm still important		

4 Coaching must develop *how*, not just *what*, ie it does not help much to say 'Work on your closing techniques' (what). Show how to do it by practice role plays (very powerful), projects, discussion, mini-quizzes. Vary each method of learning to create interest.

5 Coaching follows this *learning model*:

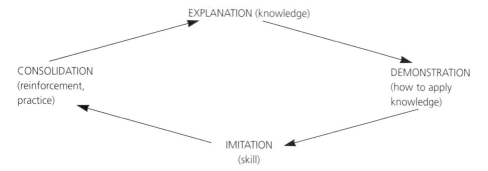

EXPLANATION (knowledge)

CONSOLIDATION
(reinforcement,
practice)

DEMONSTRATION
(how to apply
knowledge)

IMITATION
(skill)

6 Coaching aims to change *behaviour*. At the end of any coaching session, the key question is: 'Will the trainee change behaviour as a result of the session?' This will not happen if you take over the call or 'show off'. Sometimes you must even risk loss of an order to allow the trainee to recover during the sales interview.

7 Before the sales call, always *plan the call* with the trainee and always *practise* (by mini role play, discussion, demonstration) before the call. This reinforces learning.

8 Always *move quickly* from the observed sales interview to the skills to be developed – do not analyse specific observed situations too extensively; they are just leads into general selling skill development (again using mini practice role plays and quizzes).

9 *Focus* on a specific area of development for each coaching visit (eg handling objections). Do not try to cover a lot of different skills, knowledge or attitudes, as this will make learning harder. Ask the trainee for his/her priority needs for development (don't impose your views). Question openly, don't tell.

10 Always end on an *uplifting note*, summarising on strengths and progress made, and agree *action points* before the next coaching event.

Coaching technique is exactly the same skill as the Sales Manager needs for performance appraisal and counselling on a regular or informal basis, as the following checklist shows (Fig. 8.3).

Guidelines	Notes
1 Ensure the necessary data is available	To substantiate discussion and to keep it factual, all documents, reports, data or back-up information should be readily available for the interview.
2 Put the other person at ease	Both parties should try to be relaxed, open-minded, aware of the purpose of the meeting, committed to its purpose and be prepared to discuss things calmly and frankly. If there is undue tension or distrust much of the value of the interview will be lost.
3 Control pace and direction of interview	Both parties have a part to play to control and influence the pace and direction of the interview to keep it relevant, helpful and work-orientated.
4 Listen . . . listen . . . listen . . .	The most difficult part of the interview is for both parties to really listen to each other. Listening is more than not speaking, it is emptying the mind of preconceived ideas or prejudices. It is being willing to consider another person's point of view and if that view is better than the one previously held, being humble enough – and big enough – to accept it.
5 Don't be destructively critical	Where possible, people should be encouraged to be self-critical – critical of their own performance and motivated to improve. This approach goes a long way to remove the unnecessary conflict from the meeting.
6 Review performance systematically	It is important to stick to the facts – facts which can be substantiated and that's where the relevant back-up information comes in handy.

Figure 8.3   Performance appraisal interviewing

7	Discuss future action	This is an opportunity to discuss with one another almost on equal terms – what has been done, how it can best be done, who will do it, when and to what standard. Any suggestions put forward or agreements reached should be written down while they are still fresh in each other's mind. This becomes an action plan.
8	Be prepared to discuss potential or aspirations	The question of the individual's potential or future promotion doesn't always arise, but it is wise to be prepared for it. A person who is considered by his or her boss not to be ready for promotion may feel he or she has the right to know the reason why not, and may expect suggestions which might improve his or her potential.
9	Identify essential training/ development required	The final part of the interview is usually devoted to discussing the training and counselling which may be required in order to carry out the agreed action plan. This should also be written down – what essential training or development is needed?; will it be given on the job or elsewhere?; who will give it and when?
10	Avoid obvious pitfalls	Such things as: – talking too much and hogging the conversation – introducing unnecessary conflict – jumping to hasty conclusions – unjustly blaming others, particularly those who are not present to defend themselves – expecting the impossible – like wanting a person to change significant character traits overnight – and lastly, making promises which neither party may be able to keep.

Coaching control

The last step to successful sales management as a coach is to control the process by recording progress against agreed standards (the last of the '3 R's' – Recognition). This is now a well-established sales management method, but some companies are still very reluctant to use such techniques due either to their own fears or to the belief that sales staff 'would not like it'.

Research shows that such recording of ASK development is welcomed by nearly all sales personnel, due to its achievement/recognition values, as long as it is used in such a way.

The method works by defining the main elements of the selling job and grouping them into categories. A rating scale is established, usually of three or four levels, eg

    1 = below standard

    2 = standard

    3 = above standard

    4 = exceptional

These definitions can be explained by a separate guide, so scores can be given fairly.

At each coaching visit the Sales Manager completes with the salesperson a checklist at the end of the visit. This reviews progress on the day, and allows the salesperson to discuss scores.

An example is given in Fig. 8.4.

It is best to **weight** the categories in order of importance by allocating points to each element out of 100. The rating (eg 1-3) times the weight gives the score, and the Sales Manager can compare scores across sales personnel to see if general training needs exist, or focus on the most important needs for each individual.

ON-GOING PERSONAL SKILLS RECORD	Name _____ By using the Performance Standards as a guide, rate performance under the following headings: 3 Above standard 2 Standard 1 Needs Attention							
DATE								
1 PLANNING PREPARATION								
a	Information							
b	Sales Tools							
c	Action Plan							
d	Call Objectives							
2	**OPENING**							
a	Opening Remarks							
b	Sales Aids							
3	**PRESENTATION**							
a	Product Knowledge							
b	Selling Points							
c	Buyer Benefits							
d	Sales Aids							
e	Handling Objections							
f	Open Questions							
g	Listening							
4	**CLOSING THE SALE**							
a	Buying Signals							
b	Method of Close							
c	Departure Drill							
5	**CALL ANALYSIS**							
a	Records/Reports							
b	Correspondence							
c	Information							
d	Self Analysis							
6 TERRITORY MANAGEMENT								
a	Use of Selling Time							
b	Competitors' Activities							
c	Territory Development							
7	**PERSONAL**							
a	Appearance							
b	Attitude							
c	Car							
8 CUSTOMER KNOWLEDGE								
a	Customer Knowledge (Wider Aspects)							
b	People Seen							
c	Customer (Group) Presentations							
	TOTAL							

At the end of each coaching day, the Divisional Sales Manager should complete this form with the sales person, discussing the various areas where improvement is necessary in relation to the day's work. The DSM should give recommendations and guidance on how the agreed weakness should be improved.

Figure 8.4   Example of skills record
Source: GTE Sylvania Ltd

		Salesperson 1		Salesperson 2		Salesperson 3		Salesperson 4	
	% weighting	score*	rating*	score*	rating*	score*	rating*	score*	rating*
Midlands Region Sales Force									
SELLING									
Rapport	3	6	2	3	1	6	2	9	3
Presentation	25	50	2	25	1	50	2	50	2
Objections	3	3	1	3	1	9	3	6	2
Conversions	11	33	3	22	2	22	2	11	1
Close/ Agreement	4	12	3	4	1	8	2	8	2
Product Knowledge	4	12	3	8	2	8	2	4	1
	50%	116		65		103		88	
ADMINISTRATION									
Call plan	10	20	2	10	1	20	2	10	1
Journey plan	7	7	1	7	1	7	1	14	2
Reporting	10	30	3	20	2	10	1	10	1
Customer Records	1	2	2	1	1	1	1	2	2
Communications Head Office Reg. Manager	10	30	3	20	2	20	2	20	2
Market Info. Pricing Trends Availability	12	36	3	24	2	12	1	12	1
	50%	125		82		70		68	
	100%	241		147		173		156	

Rating
1 = below standard   * Score = weight × rating
2 = standard
3 = above standard

Figure 8.5   Example of how skills records can be used with weighting method

Figure 8.5 is an example from another company, with different skill categories, using this weighting method.

(a) In this example, we can see that 'Presentation' is easily the most important quality (25 per cent weighting). For salesperson 2, this is a priority for development (below standard on the most important quality).

(b) Three of the four sales staff are below standard for the job (which is a rating of 2 100 = *200* points).

(c) Areas like 'Journey planning' and 'Customer records' are below standard on average across the team – this could be the basis of a group training session at a sales meeting.

(d) This company weighted 'Selling' and 'Administration' as of equal importance. This is unusual, and could be reviewed with the sales team. Also, the qualities themselves may be reviewed, eg there are no attitude qualities being assessed.

The key points to remember when using coaching records are:

1 The method is designed to motivate by achievement/recognition, not to use as a stick.

2 Involve the sales team in the process and design of the form.

3 Gain self-completion by the individual and discuss only if they are being too easy on themselves (often they will be too self-critical).

4 Use it only for coaching – it is not a formal appraisal device.

5 Review categories weighting and standards definition regularly.

6 Keep it simple in terms of category headings – one company had 67 items on their form, which is impractical for coaching.

7 Be trained in how to coach – it is a core Sales Manager skill.

CHECKPOINTS

- How can the clarity, frequency and methods of sales coaching be improved?
- How can the quality of each coaching field visit be improved?
- How can your skills record be developed to evaluate ASK improvement?

—————— CHAPTER NINE ——————

Sales meetings

Sales meetings are extremely important dates in the Manager's calendar. They provide an opportunity for motivation, training, objective setting, planning and control.

They should be equally important for the sales force, providing practical help, direction, team spirit, and a definite commitment to the Company. Too often they are poorly conducted, and become boring chores for the team.

Administration

How often and when?

Meetings have four main objectives.

(i) to relate sales results to action planning;

(ii) to train and develop the team;

(iii) to build enthusiasm and motivation;

(iv) to improve communications.

Frequency will vary from industry to industry and also depend on such things as sales-force spread, subjects to be covered, etc.

There is no point in holding a meeting simply because four weeks have elapsed since the last one, but monthly is a sensible frequency for most sales forces.

However, if the business has a regular pattern, the chances are that the manager will wish to influence the conduct of future operations. Thus he/she will normally hold meetings as part of the pattern, eg monthly, quarterly. Objectives will also determine when in the period to hold the meeting. If it is to analyse results he/she will hold it as soon as they are available. If it is to influence actions next period, it will be held sufficiently ahead to permit adequate planning. Normally, he/she wants to do both and the middle of the month is about the best time.

Who should take part?

The people whom he/she wishes to influence should be the participants. Try to minimise or keep out observers. If senior managers wish to appraise the person running the meeting they can check preparation and analyse afterwards, although observing a meeting can provide a good coaching opportunity.

Length?

It is most productive to allow a full day, with a training session (up to half a day) at most meetings. A late-morning start and mid-afternoon finish are rarely productive uses of time.

Preparation

Content

The sequence of preparation used by many successful managers is as follows:

(a) Keep a file of meeting points:
- Points arising from previous meetings.
- Previous action plans.
- Sales results analysis.

(b) Review the information in the file:
- Decide which items must be covered and amount of time needed.
- List all other possible items and time requirements.
- Select the ones to be included.
- Decide how to handle those that cannot be included, eg memo, telephone call.

(c) For each item to be included:
- Set an action-based objective.
- Note the essence of the message.

 – Main points to be made.

 – Methods to be used, eg lecture, role play, discussion, practical exercises, films, guest speaker.

(d) Decide on the sequence.

(e) Prepare the agenda.

 – Avoid any other business.

 – Circulate.

Conduct

- **Opening**
  – Welcome the team.
  – Introduce any guests.
  – State the overall objectives and theme.
  – Explain how the objectives will be achieved:
    – Sessions.
    – Reasons.
  – Any questions before the meeting begins.

- **General guidelines**

  Atmosphere is extremely important at a meeting. The manager wants positive, thoughtful contributions. Therefore:

  – There are no 'right' answers unless they are facts.
  – Never reject 'wrong' answers out of hand.
  – No attacks on individuals. Do it privately or let the group do it, but constructively. Avoid round the table sales results presentations (quickly boring, and often demotivational).
  – Encourage comment.
  – Treat all comments seriously.

- **Guest speakers**
  – Introduce the speaker:
    Name.
    Title of the subject.
    Why that speaker.
  – Don't discuss the subject before he or she has spoken.

Checklist for chairing meetings

- Friendly? ☐
- Break the ice? ☐
- Discussion leader, not lecturer? ☐
- Hold back own opinion? ☐
- Unprejudiced; fair to all? ☐
- Patient? ☐
- Enthusiastic? ☐
- Did questions provoke thought? ☐
- Meeting topic properly introduced? ☐
- Yes/no questions avoided? ☐
- Problem worded properly? ☐
- Guiding not driving position? ☐
- Watch trend and interject stimulating remarks? ☐
- Clarify and/or illustrate important points? ☐
- Refer questions back to group; not answer myself? ☐
- Discourage useless and/or damaging discussion? ☐
- Tactfully draw out the shy or reserved? ☐
- Tactfully handle the talkative? ☐
- Discussion kept to the point? ☐
- Individual participation secured (including chairing of sessions by team members)? ☐
- Every relevant suggestion acknowledged? ☐
- Discussion kept moving towards goal? And open until all facts in? ☐
- New topics offered when old exhausted? ☐
- Did I summarise? ☐
- Fast and clear overhead projector/flip chart work? ☐
- Did discussion cover as much ground as practicable? ☐

Sales meeting planning list

General Facilities	Room Size	Delegate Requirements
Location	Layout	Notepaper
Overnight accomm.	Chairs	Binders
Eating arrangements	Tables	Pencils
Charging and	Lighting	Rubbers
invoicing	Ventilation	Name badges
arrangements	Electrical sockets	
Telephones	Window blinds	
Cloakrooms	Ashtrays	
Message handling	Water and glasses	
	Projector/flip charts	
Agenda	*Refreshments Audience*	
Items requested	Morning coffee	Selected
Theme	Lunch	Notified
Finalised	Afternoon tea	Briefed
Circulated		Visitors

Sales meeting – session examples

	Example 1 *(Research use)*	*Example 2* (Training)
Session objectives	to increase knowledge of research techniques; to improve ability in use of research in selling	Improve objection-handling skill
Content	Definition of market research Basic methods Interpreting results	Resumé of techniques practice
Method	Lecture/discussion	Film; role playing
Visual aids	Overhead projector with prepared slides	16mm projector and screen, CCTV.

Handouts	Session notes	Notes on techniques with
	Copy of latest survey	examples
Timing	90 minutes	Film: 30 minutes
		Discussion: 30 minutes
		Role playing: 60 minutes
Speaker	Market Research	Sales Manager
	Manager	
Chairman	Sales Manager	Senior Sales Executive

20 practical ideas for better meetings

1 Concentrate Agenda on *action* (future), not *communication* of results (history). Rough guideline: 75 per cent action planning, 25 per cent communications (time allocation, excluding training).

2 *Pre-circulate* sales results to team, and any basic information, so that time is minimised on factual communication.

3 *Pre-brief* team on objectives (output) and requirements from them (input) for each topic (eg 'Come with six ideas on . . .').

4 *Shorter* topic timings (attention span).

5 Stay *enthusiastic* and keep *pace* lively throughout, avoiding negative or demotivational methods (e.g. fun forfeits for negative comments).

6 *Record* all ideas (flip chart).

7 Vary *methods* to produce lots of creative ideas in a fun atmosphere (e.g. prizes for good ideas).

8 *Split team* up to produce action points during the meeting, rather than discuss from front all the time.

9 Sales Manager (if Chairman) should be *neutral* during discussions.

10 Create *ownership* of ideas by team/individuals (eg syndicate groups).

11 *Never criticise* individuals at meetings for poor performance (eg round table discussion of performance) – do this privately – but *praise* good performance.

12 Keep to *timings* (don't digress).

13 *Focus/package* ideas from group.

14 Recap/*summarise* next stage of discussion and actions agreed.

15 Develop an involvement/asking/selling *style* – don't tell.

16 Keep strong members under *control*, and involve the weaker contributors.

17 *Check* around the group before deciding.

18 Always include a *training* session in a Sales Meeting to develop knowledge or skill or attitudes, and learn which methods best develop ASK.

19 Keep *minutes* short, action-orientated, and immediate.

20 *Evaluate success* at running meetings – use the Meetings Criteria as a questionnaire, and act on feedback.

Sales meetings – seven criteria

Ask for feedback occasionally after sales meetings by getting each team member to score you (out of ten) on each of the criteria. Act on the results.

METHODS used	(varied)
UPLIFTING	(motivational/enthusiasm)
STRUCTURED	(agenda, timings etc.)
INVOLVEMENT	(everyone included)
CREATIVE	(number/quality of ideas)
ACTION	(clarity of agreed action)
LEADER'S STYLE	(asking, not telling)

Training at sales meetings

The principles discussed in Chapter 8 should lead the Sales Manager to incorporate 'off-the-job' training sessions at most sales meetings. This will give more emphasis to the '3 Rs':

– Repetition
– Reinforcement
– Recognition.

Method	Develop knowledge?	Develop skills?	Change attitudes?	Provide feedback?
1. Lecture	Yes, especially valuable for technical subjects such as products.	No	Can do if used skilfully	No – except body language
2. Participative discussions	Yes, uses knowledge of whole group	No	Yes, but can set up resistance if part of group is too strongly persuasive	Yes
3. Demonstration by Trainer (and video examples)	Yes, especially if used to support lecture or discussion	Not directly	Yes, but confident and too perfect demonstrations can demoralise delegates	No
4. Role playing	Yes, especially following a mix of 1, 2 and 3 above	Yes, the best skill development technique in off-the-job training	Yes, allows experience and success. But some people are against role play and resistance can be destructive	No
5. Practical exercises	Yes, valuable reinforcement of knowledge given in 1, 2 and 3	Yes	Yes, experience and success	Yes
6. Questionnaire and tests	Not directly – but discussion over the answers can	Not directly	Success can reassure. Failure might cause resentment	Yes, valuable especially for product and technical subjects
7. Interactive video systems with trainer support	Yes	Yes, if material well prepared	Yes, can build confidence	Yes
8. Case studies	Yes, valuable reinforcement of knowledge gained in 1, 2 and 3	Some, particularly in areas of analysis and decision taking	Yes, but 'case' material needs to be realistic and to be taken seriously by delegates and trainers	Yes

Figure 9.1   Sales development methods of Sales Managers

Off-the-job training methods

Those techniques which are applicable to sales training are:

1 Lecture.

2 Participative discussion.

3 Practical exercises.

4 Demonstration.

5 Role-playing.

6 Quizzes/tests.

None of these headings is exclusive. Almost all training activities combine several techniques. Indeed, the more successful the training, the more blurred the distinction becomes between methods. (See Fig. 9.1)

1. Lecture

Formal presentation by the trainer of information and concepts with or without the use of audio/visual aids.

Appropriate:

- For large groups of well motivated listeners.
- For presentation of factual information.
- Where for any reason discussion must be avoided.
- Where time is a prime limitation.
- Where the objective is to inspire, entertain or stimulate.
- To introduce a subject for later analysis in detail.

Attributes:

- Enables large amount of information to be presented in shortest time.
- Places no limit on audience size.
- Acceptable to a wide range of speakers.

Remember:

- Retention of lectured information will be low if not reinforced by later discussion.
- Interpretation of information will vary widely.
- Feedback is minimal.
- No lecture should be given without breaks or audio/visual support.
- If lectures are used, use the time at the start of training.

2. Participative discussion

Exchange of information, views, ideas and experiences within the training group, led and structured by the trainer.

Appropriate:

- For small groups.
- Where initial trainee motivation is low.
- Where the objective is learning, understanding and retention.
- Where the aim is to change attitudes.
- For all conceptual subjects.
- Where solutions are sought.
- Where concepts and principles need to be established.
- Analysis of information.

Attributes:

- Feedback informs and guides content and presentation.
- Facts can be set to enable common understanding.
- Disagreements and problems can be identified and resolved.
- Trainer learns from trainees.
- The whole group can pool experience and enhance their individual knowledge.
- Participation gives commitment through involvement.

Remember:

- It is the best method of presentation for Sales Training.

- But requires a high degree of skill to be effective.

- Take time to maintain the structure of the discussion.

- Plan, and use, open-ended questions to stimulate discussion: Who? Why? What? Where? How?

3. Practical exercise

Completion by individuals or groups of a task set by the trainer.

Appropriate:

- For breaking up long formal sessions.

- To stimulate thought and analysis.

- To illustrate concepts.

- To change, challenge or analyse attitudes.

- To introduce a competitive element.

- To enable content to be assimilated.

- For producing planned feedback.

- To practise and develop mental or manual skills.

Attributes:

- Full involvement and activity by trainees.

- Simultaneous feedback.

- Can combine demonstration and role-playing.

- Enables learning by discovering.

- Nearly always welcomed by all trainees.

Remember:

- Takes time to do well.

- Needs careful preparation to achieve right level of complexity, ie relevant to subject but related to trainees' experience and easy to interpret for success.

4. Demonstration

Demonstration of skills, ideas, techniques by the trainer, (including use of films or pre-prepared video examples).

Appropriate:

- Where a 'live' illustration is necessary.
- As a preliminary to role-playing.
- Where a skill is being taught, eg the use of visual aids.
- Where it is necessary or desirable for the trainer to establish his/her own competence.

Attributes:

- Can be convincing and memorable.
- Can add light relief to dull topics.
- Enhances the value of later or previous learning.
- Enables standards to be established.

Remember:

- Needs a high degree of skill.
- If done too well may dazzle rather than train.
- If muffed it may reinforce prejudice or affect credibility.
- Can demoralise the slow learners or the very inexperienced.

5. Role-playing

Simulation by trainees of face-to-face selling or communication situation.

Appropriate:

- For training in selling skills.

- To enable group learning through observation and practice.

- For trying out new skills, techniques or ideas.

- For correcting bad habits and encouraging good ones.

Attributes:

- Gets close to reality without the risk of practising skills on customers.

- Is the only successful way of changing habits outside the work situation.

- Helps to fix knowledge and attitude changes, as well as skills.

- Enables trainer to develop the learning started by other methods and link off-job with on-job training.

Remember:

- Results can mislead you (some trainees become 'professional' role players).

- Requires time and resources.

- Needs a high degree of skill and patience.

Methods of role-playing

Role-playing works best if:

(a) Video is used, to allow play-back/analysis.

(b) Real situations, developed by participants, are used (not invented situations).

(c) The Sales Manager observes, and allows others to take part/analyse.

(d) Screens separate participants from observers.

(e) De-brief follows good coaching practice (as in Chapter 8).

(f) Observers focus on separate parts of the sales interview.

(g) Everyone takes part.

(h) It is emphasised as a learning experience, not a criticism of individuals.

6. Quizzes/texts

This is a core method of testing knowledge, especially product knowledge.

Quizzes/tests can be used during all training methods, eg role play de-brief. An example would be: 'Give me four typical objections and how would you handle them?' They are a key part of reinforcement/repetition learning and should be used frequently.

In some sales forces (notably financial services), quizzes/tests are used to assess competence levels, and staff are not allowed to sell products unless minimum scores are obtained.

Conclusion

Sales Meetings are often seen by the sales force as a rest day, an interference in earning capacity, or a waste of time. This is all down to the way they are conducted. Many of the ideas covered in this Chapter are not carried out due to poor planning and implementation by the Sales Manager, and by an adherence to traditional ways of conducting sales meetings which are too heavy on one-way communication and too light on training and action-planning in a motivational way.

CHECKPOINTS

- How can the planning of agendas be improved at Sales Meetings to focus more on action planning than communications?

- How can sales meetings be conducted to create more motivational impact?

- How can sales meetings be used more effectively for training the sales team?

CHAPTER TEN

Sales audit

Sales Managers who implement methods suggested in this book will increase their probability of success in most situations. From time to time, however, a performance problem leads to a need to review all management practices to decide on changes and improvements. This is called a sales audit.[1]

Some of the *reasons for poor performance* might be:

(a) Changes in customer needs, buying power and concentration.

(b) Cost escalation relative to sales volume.

(c) Technology changes offering new opportunities, eg telemarketing; electronic ordering; computerised data capture.

(d) Skills shortages.

(e) Changing selling job roles, eg from order taker to service provider.

(f) Organisational strains due to new methods of market, customer and product segmentation.

(g) Needs to change the culture, eg from administration or production orientation to customer-led focus.

(h) New customer service/total quality requirements.

(i) Changes in organisational culture, eg from top-down, autocratic styles to bottom-up empowered cultures.

(j) Competitive changes not responded to effectively.

[1] Some references in this Chapter are drawn from *Sales Force Management in Europe*, 1986, the Economist Intelligence Unit.

Who should do it and how often?

Sales audits are least successful when carried out by Sales Managers too quickly and based on intuition or prejudice.

As one Sales Director put it:

'A sales force may be slumping for dozens of different reasons. No matter how good your instincts on these matters are, you never know what's wrong until you take the trouble to find out. The worst thing you can do is to start fixing things before finding out what's wrong with them. Yet that's what so many companies do.'

Increasingly, specialist management consultants are asked to carry out sales audits, often in conjunction with internal teams. Consultants benefit from:

(a) Objective viewpoints, with no internal prejudices.

(b) Experience of similar situations in other companies.

(c) Creative ideas for change.

(d) Cost-effective solutions, eg by immediate cost savings, or revenue increases.

(e) Credibility of recommended actions particularly with senior management.

There is a strong case for regular sales audits, regardless of perceptions of major problems existing at the time. Even small improvements can add to performance and sales audits show scope for improvement even in units performing well. Performance may be good but is it as good as it could be?

Regular sales audits are carried out by successful Sales Managers in successful companies.

Narrow and wide audits

While wide reviews of all aspects of sales management may be desirable, the costs and time involved are very high.

A narrow area of focus may be the best place to start, even though performance is rarely down to one area only.

Thus an audit might focus on:

- Training/coaching.
- Motivation.
- Pay/commission.
- Planning/control.
- Organisation.
- Customer service.

The narrow audit may spread out to other areas, but if it is the root of the problem, much time and effort will be saved by taking this route.

Involvement

Audits rarely succeed if they are not 'sold' properly to the sales team, or do not involve them in the scope for analysis.

Resentment may surface that the audit only wants to 'snoop' or 'fault find'. If the sales team are involved right at the start in setting out purpose and methodology, and are involved in the project discussions, the audit should enthuse the team, not demoralise it.

Sales audit stages

The stages will depend on the objectives and scope of the audit, but typical stages would be:

Stage 1. Information collection

This would be a full understanding of what is currently done in every part of the selling job. Typical information collected would include:

- Job descriptions.
- Job standards.
- Recruitment methods (profiles, checklists, etc).
- Sales plan formats.
- Sales control forms.

- Organisation charts.
- Coaching forms.
- Meeting agendas.
- Sales results over time, by salesperson, market, product, etc.

If possible competitive information for comparison would be collected.

Stage 2. Market analysis

As customer needs drive business decisions, market research is often commissioned to discover attitudes, feelings, competitive comparisons, preferences, etc.

This avoids reliance by sales management on intuition or prejudice, and can often produce alarming information. In one example, a company thought it had the best sales service standards, while customers rated it worst of all suppliers in this area.

Customer surveys can be very expensive depending on methods used, but any market-focused company should regard customer opinions as a vital part of its data base.

Stage 3. Internal staff interviews

A sample of sales staff should be interviewed to obtain their opinions on a range of issues within the scope of the audit.

These interviews can be individual or group discussion based, but should follow pre-set checklists to ensure consistency.

Stage 4. Field accompaniment

A sample of sales staff should be accompanied on normal visits to customers to observe what happens in a 'snap-shot' of field activity. Subjects covered would be as in field coaching (eg skills; time use; territory and customer planning) and the visits would allow time for interviews to supplement those in Stage 3.

Stage 5. Analysis

All information collected can be analysed into pre-set pro formas for sales and market analysis and qualitative conclusions.

Good examples of the latter would be strengths and weaknesses; opportunities and threats; views of the Company culture and motivation.

Stage 6. Brainstorming

The team should now be involved in brainstorming solutions to perceived problems, often facilitated by consultants (these sessions are often called workshops).

This creates ownership and involvement, and avoids the danger of solutions created by 'outsiders' and imposed on the staff.

Stage 7. Action planning/implementation

Following the workshop stage, sub-teams of sales staff can be made responsible for specific project action plans. They would work on courses of action and report back to a project leader (the Sales Manager or a consultant).

Their ideas can then be 'test marketed' and evaluated to judge success.

Stage 8. Review

After a suitable period, the results of actions taken as a result of the audit should be reviewed.

This is often done by creating more team workshops to discuss results and arrive at further improvements. Again, these sessions are often facilitated by consultants.

Questioning

Sales Audits require extensive questioning of current procedures. The following is a typical set of questions:[1]

1. Organisation

(a) How many sales staff do we have/need?

(b) What would be the effect on sales of cutting/increasing the sales force?

---

[1] Some questions are drawn from A. Wilson, *Checklists Guide to Effective Marketing*, McGraw-Hill, 1982.

(c) How are they organised by region, by industry/application, by type of customer, by product/service, etc.?

(d) Are the reasons for this form of organisation still valid?

(e) Are spans of control effective?

2. Customers

(a) What are customer needs from the sales force?

(b) How do we satisfy those needs?

(c) How do we compare competitively?

(d) Would meeting customer needs be incompatible with our needs?

3. Pay

(a) What method of remuneration are we using?

(b) How does it differ from previous methods?

(c) Why were the present methods adopted?

(d) What proof do we have that it provides strong motivation?

(e) How does our remuneration method compare with competitors?

(f) Can we justify any differences?

(g) Have we considered alternative methods?

(h) What other benefits do our sales force get?

(i) Would there be a stronger/weaker motivation if benefits were revised?

(j) Is our pay system consistent with the selling job?

4. Motivation

(a) Rate the motivation of the sales force: high, moderate, low.

(b) Is motivation rising or falling?

(c) What major factors provide motivation in each sales team member?

(d) Is our company culture helping or hindering motivation?

(e) Are motivations understood and actioned?

(f) How good are our Sales Managers at motivation?

5. Recruitment

(a) How are the sales force recruited?

(b) What is the record of sales force turnover?

(c) How does it compare with the standard for the industry?

(d) What is the major cause of losses?

(e) How far can losses be attributed to poor recruitment criteria and methods?

(f) Can any of our recruitment methods be improved?

6. Planning control

(a) What criteria are used for performance evaluation and how frequently is an evaluation made?

(b) Do the sales force know and understand the criteria used for judging the performance?

(c) Are the criteria valid in today's conditions?

(d) What targets do the sales force have?

(e) Do targets include performance ratios as well as absolute standards?

(f) Are they reached in agreement with the sales force?

(g) If not, is the method of arriving at a target explained to the sales force?

(h) How does each salesperson perform against target?

(i) Is constant under-performance dealt with effectively?

(j) What rewards or acknowledgements do they receive for passing targets?

(k) Is there a report-back system so that they can compare their performance with others or with the best and with the firm's progress as a whole?

(l) What steps can we take to eliminate poor performance?

7. Training/coaching

(a) Is our induction training programme working effectively?

(b) Do we provide clear training programmes for all levels of sales staff?

(c) Is training continuous or infrequent?

(d) How often do we coach on-the-job?

(e) Do Sales Managers coach effectively?

(f) Do sales meetings have training sessions incorporated?

8. Sales service

(a) How does our sales service compare with that of competitors?

(b) How fast do we respond to customer enquiries?

(c) How good is our delivery service?

(d) How well do we handle complaints?

(e) Do our back-up/sales office systems work effectively?

(f) Is our paperwork customer-friendly?

(g) How would customers describe our service?

9. Sales meetings

(a) Do Sales Managers conduct motivational sales meetings?

(b) Do sales staff feel motivated /enthused at meetings?

(c) Are agendas effective?

(d) Do we need to train and action plan more, and administer less?

(e) Do we evaluate meeting success?

These are just some of the questions which sales audits can address. Any one area may be creating significant performance problems, so regular audits should more than return their time and cost investment and help to 'grow' sales management skills.

Honest feedback

- How effective are your Sales Management personal skills?

- Are your perceptions of how the Sales team view you accurate?

- Are you prepared to find out?

One of the main reasons for poor Sales Force performance lies in the lack of personal skills of Sales Managers. These skills need to be assessed regularly so any necessary corrective action can be taken.

In principle, good Sales Managers should be able to ask regularly for honest feedback from their team members and expect it to be given. In practice, there are a number of *problems* to overcome.

1 The Sales Manager is often unaware of any problem areas due to a false self-image, believing skills are good (or even excellent) when they may not be seen that way by the team.

2 The Sales Manager is aware of problem areas, but is reluctant to ask for feedback for reasons of self-esteem and status with the team. This attitude only succeeds in building up problems for the future, and frustrates Manager/Team relationships.

3 The team members may not give honest feedback to the Sales Manager (whether invited or not), due to concerns about job security, politics, appraisal, career development etc. No matter how open a Sales Manager wishes to be, team members may not be willing to give honest feedback directly (or even by anonymous questionnaire methods). When feedback is given, it may be framed in terms that the Sales Manager 'wants to hear', rather than in full honesty.

If these problems exist, the only *solution* may be to use an independent facilitator, either within the Company (eg Personnel specialist), or an outside Consultant. The benefit of using Consultants for this purpose is that people will talk much more freely and will give more honest feedback to those with no vested interest and who are seen to be outside the Company's political structure. Coaching and mentoring are also easier via independent facillitators. The following is an example of a Sales Management Feedback Questionnaire.

SALES MANAGEMENT FEEDBACK QUESTIONNAIRE

Manager . . . .

Skill Area	Rating (1–5)	Relative Importance *Example*	Relative Importance
1 Motivation		8	
2 Style of management		2	
3 Leadership			
4 Sales planning		4	
5 Sales meetings		1	
6 Coaching/training		2	
7 Counselling/advice			
8 Appraisal			
9 Communication		3	
10 Support			
11 Team spirit			
12 Feedback			
13 Personal development			
14 Creative thinking			
15 Negotiations with staff			
		20 points	20 points

RATING KEY:
1 = very poor
2 = poor
3 = acceptable
4 = good
5 = very good

In this column, please allocate 20 points to the top 6 Skill Areas to indicate how much importance you attach to each.
In the example, Motivation is rated the most important item, receiving 8 points, etc.

A score will be calculated by multiplying the rating for each of the 6 key skill areas by the 'relative importance' weight. This will give a maximum score for each respondent of 100 (5 maximum rating points × 20 relative importance points). The average score for the Sales Manager will be the total number of points achieved divided by the number of sales personnel who completed the questionnaire.

© *Grant Stewart: Langham Management Consultants*

COMMENTS

1. Please make any comments on any of the Skill Areas for your manager. These may be areas of particular strength or weakness, giving reasons or examples for your views.

2. What would you like your manager, as a sales manager, to do:

   a) More of

   b) Less of

Thank you for your help and co-operation.

CASE STUDY

An example from one Company illustrates the benefits to the Sales Manager of obtaining honest feedback from the Sales Force (feedback from staff, superiors and colleagues is known as 360° feedback).

We were asked by a Divisional Director of a large Company to investigate reasons for poor and deteriorating performance in one team. It was felt intuitively that the Regional Sales Manager concerned may be slipping in his personal skills, but no firm evidence was to hand.

On interview, the Regional Sales Manager felt that he was doing a good job, and was well liked and respected by the team. We asked if he would agree to an audit of his skills and methods by interviewing members of his team. This he was very keen to do, motivated by a desire for self-improvement (not all Sales Managers would be so keen, but therein lies the problem!).

During the day of interviews, by questionnaire and group discussion methods, with two separate groups of team members (his Area Sales Managers and Sales Force members), the following opinions emerged:

A. Area Sales Managers Group	Sales Force*				Regional Sales Manager				Divisional Management				Head Office Management			
	1	2	3	4	1	2	3	4	1	2	3	4	1	2	3	4
1. Motivation	4				1			4	3	2	1					6
2. Style of Management	4				1		3		6					6		
3. Degree of Control	4					3	1		4	1	1				5	
4. Planning	3	1				1	4		3	2					1	5
5. Meetings	3	2			3	2			1	1	1					
6. Coaching/Training	5				1		3		2	3	1			3	1	
7. Counselling/Advice	4				1		3		2	1	1					
8. Appraisal	2	1				3	1									
9. Communication	5				1	3	1		5	1			3	2	1	
10. Support	5					3	1		5		1		5	1		
11. Team Spirit		2	3		1	1	4		1	3	2				2	3
12. Feedback	5						5		6				5	1		
13. No. of Campaigns	2	4			3	2				6				6		
14. Career Development	4	1			4	2			4	2						

*'Sales Force' column is how Managers feel Sales Force will view them; other columns are as Sales Force sees their Management.

Key: 1 = Very satisfied
    2 = Satisfied
    3 = Not satisfied
    4 = Not at all satisfied.

Figure 10.1 Number who expressed an opinion on degree of satisfaction with Management's effect on each topic raised.

Conclusion

After the Report was presented, we facilitated a personal feedback session with the Regional Sales Manager. He was very shocked by the findings, but keen to agree to an Action Plan to improve his personal skills.

Within 6 months, the Region had climbed rapidly up the Company League Table of performance. It was a *'Win-Win'* situation for all concerned.

- The Regional Sales Manager had improved his personal skills and, by acting on feedback from the Team, had formed a closer bond for the future.

- The Team had been involved in a feedback process which they found motivational and rewarding.

- The Divisional Director achieved improved performance, on which he was judged.

- We were pretty happy too!

The point is that in many Sales Forces, such personal skill problems go unrecognised because honest feedback is not sought or offered regularly.

In the example given, it was a problem not perceived by the Sales Manager concerned, nor was feedback given voluntarily by Sales Team members for a variety of fear reasons.

A problem not recognised is a problem not solved. Honest feedback should be encouraged by all Sales Managers and intervention facilitation should be welcomed if honesty cannot be achieved internally.

- How effective are your Sales Management personal skills?

- Are your perceptions of how the Sales Team view you accurate?

- Are you prepared to find out?

CHECKPOINTS

- How do you review the effectiveness of your sales organisation and processes?
- How can you use 360° feedback for greater sales management effectiveness?
- How often and by what methods should sales audits be carried out?

CHAPTER ELEVEN

Achieving excellence and quality

Excellence in sales management as put forward in this book follows principles established recently by such management thinkers as Tom Peters and Rosabeth Moss Kanter.

Their research conclusions were that excellent, quality companies followed a number of well established practices.

The fact that most of these principles seemed to them to be just common sense contrasted sharply with the absence of good management in so many companies.

The following 21 principles of effective sales management will increase the chances of success for any Sales Manager:

The effective Sales Manager – qualities and actions

1 *Vision*/strategy/direction.

2 Leadership (active) – 'Managing by Walking About'.

3 *Motivation* – individuals and teams want to work for you, not forced.

4 Clear *standards of performance*/goals.

5 A *written* and *communicated* sales action plan process (bottom-up).

6 Continuous *analysis of results*/corrective action.

7 Motivational *pay/rewards*.

8 *Hands on*/concern/style/caring.

9 *Coach*/cheer leader/facilitator.

10 *Communication*/feedback.

11 *Innovator*.

12 *Close to customers* – ask them what they think/need.

13 Quality products/*service* – quality circles.

14 *Autonomy*/entrepreneurship.

15 *Productivity* through people.

16 Keep it *simple*.

17 Bias for *action*/decisive.

18 Keep *stretching* yourself and team.

19 Manage *stress* and *time*.

20 Sells, asks, *not* tells.

21 *Praise* before criticism.

The qualities identified through research, and most admired in the best managers, can be summarised as:

- Really knows the job and does it well.
- Never panics.
- Tells you exactly what is expected.
- You know precisely how you stand.
- Is fair and has neither favourites nor scapegoats.
- You felt you could never let him or her down.
- I really enjoyed working for him or her.

A number of conditions need to exist to achieve successful sales management.

1. Recruitment

Many Sales Managers are in the wrong jobs due to poor recruitment decisions. These decisions take two forms:

- *Too good at selling* – this is the 'best salesperson' problem, where promotion to sales management may be a mistake due to lack of 'people' skills. Good sales people are often selfish with high ego drives who like working alone and do not like people or relate easily to them.

- *Too weak at selling* – This is particularly a problem in industries relatively new to a sales culture, eg privatised companies, banks, building societies. Many new Sales Managers are just too weak at selling to be credible or creative as managers, and may not be able to be trained. Experienced Sales Managers may have to be imported in such situations, and in situations where the sales culture is strong but management potential is weak.

2. Company culture

Good sales management flourishes in sales cultures, and struggles where other values are dominant, eg production, finance, administration.

Sales cultures are recognised by:

- Strong customer-led values.
- Recognition for achieving sales results.
- Promotion based on strong business development elements.
- Rewards for sales results.
- Positive sales attitudes by staff.
- Top management commitment to sales values.
- Organisation based on sales, not other dominant criteria.
- Enthusiastic, motivational atmosphere.
- Participation in decision-making not imposition.
- Small spans of control to build team spirits.

3. Personal style

Many Sales Managers would be more successful if they related their style of management to sound motivational principles.

In most situations, good Sales Managers are:

- democratic;
- involving;
- listening;
- empowering;
- asking.

Poor ones are:

- dominant;
- autocratic;
- centralised;
- telling.

It is important to understand your own personality profile so you can see the difficulties you will face with certain types of people, and adapt your style accordingly. While you cannot change your personality, you can change your style.

4. Attitude/Skills/Knowledge (ASK)

Most successful Sales Managers, like sales staff, are made, not born. They are made by continuous learning through training and coaching.

It is amazing how many companies regard training as a one-off experience, eg a one week course, or an annual field visit.

The 3Rs of:

- Repetition
- Reinforcement
- Recognition

show that training never stops, and the right mix of

- off-the-job training (eg courses)
- on-the-job training (coaching)
- self-learning

will produce the best Sales Managers. In particular coaching of Sales Managers by Sales Directors is often woefully inadequate.

5. The Boss

It is hard to be a successful Sales Manager without the support and guidance of 'the Boss'. Sometimes, he/she is rarely seen and is a hindrance rather than a help.

If the Sales Manager's boss works with him or her in the same way as recommended for the sales management to work with the team, motivation will increase.

When was the last time your boss talked to you about your motivation or skills or interests or ambitions?

Often, these problems of relations with the boss come down to management style and motivational skill, but sometimes the problem could be span of control. In some companies, notably those with large branch networks, Sales Directors simply have too many managers for whom they are responsible, reducing call frequencies and producing management by memo and phone.

It is well worthwhile for Sales Managers to try to 'manage the boss' by requesting regular meetings and giving honest feedback as to how they would like to be managed. Sometimes problems of culture or status make this very difficult, but this is a sad reflection on the existence, or not, of a motivational sales culture.

11 steps to take towards successful sales management

1. Ask for feedback

Too few Sales Managers have the courage to ask their sales force for feedback on how they are doing as a Manager. They often have false perceptions of their skills or motivational abilities, and ignorance will lead to failure to change behaviour or recognise problems.

It can be beneficial to ask an objective outsider (eg consultant) to take feedback on an anonymous basis, present findings to the Sales Manager and facilitate change.

Once feedback is received, acting on the results will show listening and responsive abilities which will bind the Manager to the Team.

2. Spend more time with the sales force

This should be a continuous objective, as there are always valuable benefits in being with the sales force rather than managing remotely. Spend more time 'managing' and less time 'doing'.

The allocation of time shows the attention you wish to give to sales force activities. If you spend time coaching, you will stress the importance of skill development and encourage learning. If you devote time to sales planning, you show its importance and encourage planning when you are not there. The reverse is the case – lack of time devoted to an activity will show you do not regard it as important, so it will not be actioned by the team.

3. Review your management style/company culture

If the company needs to change its culture to a more motivational climate, this will be a long-term process, involving much change management.

An individual Sales Manager should be able to recognise which style of management is appropriate for his or her own company and team, and change if appropriate. Style and culture have a significant and increasing effect on sales management success.

4. Spend more time and create more action on motivation

While many job skills are important, motivation is the most important, and it can be learnt. Charisma helps, as does likeability, but hard work on understanding the nature of motivation and demotivation will reap rewards.

Many Sales Managers simply fail to treat motivation as an activity in itself, and devote little time to it. They become lazy at motivation, and become surprised when morale drops or people leave. The pay system needs regular review to ensure it is motivating correct behaviour in the sales force.

5. Make job standards fully clear

It is vital to set clear qualitative job standards by defining key tasks and expectations, and to keep defining and re-defining measurable standards, such as performance ratios.

Team standards and individual standards are equally important, so everyone feels the job is totally clear and 'flag-planting' exists – a continual striving for new goals.

6. Review the sales planning/control system

The way targets are set and the quality of the planning/control system can be major demotivators if perceived as unfair and undemocratic.

In a positive light, good sales planning creates a sense of shared direction which is vital to sales success. Budgeting alone should be avoided, as planning is about activities to be taken and measured, not just results.

7. Organise for sales effectiveness

Historical sales structures may be inappropriate for customer, market or product changes and may be impeding sales success. In particular, if spans of control become too large for effective management, poor team-work results.

Sales forces are a very expensive resource and need to be organised for maximum cost-effectiveness – but too many reduced costs may decimate effectiveness. Creative use of new distribution channels and remote sales methods (eg direct mail, telesales) may revolutionise sales organisations, reduce cost and actually increase coverage and effectiveness.

8. Recruit excellent sales staff

As any sports team manager will confirm, you cannot make a good team without good players. Care in recruitment will pay dividends and if a team is taken over, an audit of each member's strengths and weaknesses should establish whether any cannot be trained or motivated and therefore should be removed from the team. It is false economy to persevere too long with sales team members who will not be able to achieve set standards.

9. Coach and train continuously

Coaching and training are the most important ways to motivate and develop sales teams and should be the largest time activity of Sales Managers.

A creative mix of induction training, formal off-the-job training and, most important, coaching on-the-job will repay time and cost investment.

It is vital to appreciate the continuous nature of training, due to the way learning takes place via the '3Rs'.

– Repetition

– Reinforcement

– Recognition

Gaps appear in attitude, skill and knowledge (ASK) all the time and must be filled for current jobs, as well as development for new ones.

The relentless and repetitive processes which apply for training sales teams apply equally to sales management. It is a continuous learning process and the more each skill is practised, the 'luckier' you get!

10. Review and improve sales meetings

Sales meetings are significant motivational occasions, and should be prepared and executed with great care.

In particular, emphasis should be given to using the team to plan future actions (rather than review past results) and to training at sales meetings.

11. Review effectiveness regularly

The sales audit is not carried out often enough in most companies, perhaps with fears about cost or time. In practice, a well executed audit, perhaps using Consultants, will recover its cost very quickly.

Every effort should be made to sell the purpose of the audit to the sales force and involve them in the process, and to carry out recommendations effectively. Reports left in the drawer are no use to anyone.

Four Key Success Factors

Any sales force will work successfully if the Sales Manager can achieve the right combination of four key success factors.

1 **Sales Focus** (the quality and direction of customer contacts)

2 **Sales Activity Levels** (the quantity and productivity of customer contacts)

3 **Attitude, Skills** and **Knowledge** (ASK) development for the sales force and Sales Management (the selling and management competences)

4 **Motivation** (the feel-good factor).

Conclusion

In conclusion, sales management is an extremely difficult job because it is one of the few management jobs where the Manager rarely sees the staff. This increases the need to recruit sales management carefully and to train and develop them effectively to be able to deliver quality to the sales force.

Given this job difficulty, motivation of sales staff is the core skill and all methods and activities can be judged on the basis of: 'Do they motivate or demotivate the sales team to perform?'

While no method or style is right for all Managers on all occasions, the hope of this book is to provide practical ideas to give a reduced chance of failure and an increased chance of success. If it achieves that, it will have met its objectives.

Two final thoughts:

IF YOU DO
WHAT YOU
HAVE **ALWAYS DONE**
YOU GET
WHAT YOU
HAVE **ALWAYS GOT**

IF YOU WANT
TO MAKE A
DIFFERENCE,
YOU HAVE TO
DO SOME THINGS
DIFFERENTLY

CHECKPOINTS

- How would you assess your effectiveness as a Sales Manager?
- What are your most important priorities for action?
- What would be your Development Plan for improved effectiveness?

Index